ECOLOGY AND RELIGION:

Toward a New
Christian Theology of Nature

JOHN CARMODY

PAULIST PRESS † *New York/Ramsey*

Library of Congress
Catalog Card Number: 82-62412

ISBN: 0-8091-2526-9

Published by Paulist Press
545 Island Road, Ramsey, N.J. 07446

Printed and bound in the
United States of America

CONTENTS

PREFACE   1

Introduction: A DRAMATIC SCENARIO   3

Part One: THE RECENT DIALOGUE BETWEEN
              ECOLOGY AND RELIGION   9
Chapter One: ISSUES FROM NATURAL SCIENCE   11
Chapter Two: TECHNOLOGICAL AND ECONOMIC
                 ISSUES   25
Chapter Three: POLITICAL AND ETHICAL ISSUES   39
Chapter Four: RELIGIOUS ISSUES   53

Part Two: TOWARD A NEW CHRISTIAN
              THEOLOGY OF NATURE   67
Chapter Five: FOUNDATIONAL REFLECTIONS   69
Chapter Six: BIBLICAL DOCTRINES   84
Chapter Seven: TRADITIONAL THEOLOGICAL
                  DOCTRINES   100
Chapter Eight: A SYSTEMATIC APPROACH   116
Chapter Nine: ETHICAL IMPLICATIONS   132
Chapter Ten: IMPLICATIONS FOR SPIRITUALITY   148

SUMMARY AND CONCLUSION   164
ANNOTATED BIBLIOGRAPHY   170
NOTES   175

DEDICATION

For John Duryea
Priest-Ecologist

PREFACE

This book started out to be a report on what the environmentalists and theologians have been saying recently about ecology. Along the way, however, it broadened its scope, becoming a full introduction to the new Christian theology of nature that the crises of the late twentieth century seem to demand. In making the transition to a full introduction, I have drawn on the work of Bernard Lonergan, perhaps the foremost of our contemporary methodologists. Specifically, I have adapted Lonergan's sketch of the functional specialties into which theology should divide so as to provide both a phase of listening and a phase of speaking.

Part One, entitled "The Recent Dialogue Between Ecology and Religion," is mainly listening. More exactly, it is an effort to hear the dialectical overtones to the debate between environmentalists and religionists. For Lonergan, a theology mediates between a given culture and the role a religion plays in that culture. After one researches, interprets, and grasps the history of a particular cultural issue, religious questions come into view in "dialectics": the debate about the ultimate horizon or value-framework in terms of which an issue finally should be cast. Part One has a rather dialectical character. Looking at our environmental crises, ecologists and religionists recently have been debating the deeper questions of outlook, worldview, or ultimate assumptions. In Part One I try to insert the reader into this debate, providing enough empirical information and sampling of viewpoints to let him or her overhear the recent arguments.

Part Two, entitled "Toward a New Christian Theology of

Nature," is more constructive or original. Continuing to use Lonergan's model, I speak about the foundations, doctrinal bases, systematic coherence, and practical aspects of a new Christian theology of nature adequate to our present ecological needs. Thus Part Two lays out the new vision of nature that a Christian religious conversion could provide, polls the biblical and traditional theologies of nature that still demand respect, suggests a new design for organizing the main doctrinal points that appear valid, and tries to put into common sense terms the practical implications this design would have for Christian ethics and spirituality.

To say the least, it is an ambitious project, so I would have the reader underscore the word "Toward" that appears in the sub-title. The most I hope to accomplish is to lay out a path, suggest an enterprise, point *toward* a new Christian theology of nature. Ideally, future theologies of nature, or any other significant topic, will be the product of teamwork. For each area that my chapters represent, the ideal would be the sort of competence only a lifetime of scholarship can assemble. In no way, therefore, do I pretend that this set of reports and reflections is more than a sketch. I will be content if it stimulates others to do better. If it stimulates others to collaborate as a team, I will be downright delighted. At the moment, though, we need new blueprints. Not having a perfectionist temperament, I'm willing to attempt one. This seems a good work for today. Tomorrow can take care of itself.

My thanks to Larry Boadt of Paulist Press, my wife Denise Lardner Carmody, and Karla Kraft for good advice and kindly collaboration.

Introduction:
A DRAMATIC SCENARIO

Our first thesis is that ecological issues are among the most pressing that the global community now faces. Technically, ethically, and religiously, we are confronted by a cluster of interlocking problems that threaten the very matrix of life, threaten humanity's very future. Perhaps the best way to launch our study, and to assure the reader that this estimate of the ecological situation is not mere hyperbole, is to present a case study, a dramatic scenario in which one can see, all too vividly, the dismal future awaiting people who don't solve their ecological crises.

Cubatao, Brazil, is one of Latin America's leading petrochemical centers, resting atop coastal lowlands intersected by four lifeless rivers. Most days Cubatao is enshrouded in a deadly mist, fed by the 1,000 or so tons of toxic gases trapped by the 2,000 foot range of hills rising up nearby. The city has about 80,000 inhabitants, but neither its mayor nor many of its officials will live in it. They apparently were willing to live in Cubatao if they were allowed to wear gas masks, but higher-ups deemed this impolitic. The prospect of citizens confronting officials outfitted in gas masks did not sit well with the state fathers and industrial officials who have the larger say in Cubatao's destiny.

Of every 1,000 babies born in Cubatao, 40 are dead at birth and another 40 perish within a week. This is at least eight times the infant mortality level in the United States (which itself does not have the world's lowest rate). Moreover, most of Cubatao's dead infants are manifestly deformed, and a number of the infants who survive are either deformed or seriously weakened. In effect, the babies are contaminated in the womb and break down, just as a pollution monitoring machine set up in 1975 broke down in 1977 because of the intensity of contamination to which it was exposed. Before breaking down, however, the machine indicated that residents of Cubatao were showered with 1,200 particulates per cubic meter of air. That is more than twice the amount the World Health Organization has said produces "excess mortality" after 24 hours.

More precisely, atmospheric tests indicated that each day Cubatao's 50 square mile area was bombarded by about 473 tons of carbon monoxide, 182 tons of sulfur dioxide, 148 tons of particulate matter, 41 tons of nitrogen oxide, and 31 tons of hydrocarbons. The giant foundry of the Paulista Steel Company was the largest polluter, but other Brazilian firms, the American firms Dow Chemical, Du Pont, and Union Carbide, and French and German firms all contributed. The pollution of Cubatao therefore has international causes. It is a good example of the complex way Northern technologies and economies are changing the face of Southern landscapes for the worse.

Cubatao has become sufficiently infamous to have made the wire services, and the newspaper report from which I gathered my statistics included some descriptive color: "Smoke rolls forth from scores of stacks in blue, yellow, red, charcoal and white, turning the air a jaundiced gray and invading the nostrils with a sickening mixture of acrid odors. There are no birds and no insects, and when it rains on particularly windless days, the drops burn the skin. The industries of Cubatao have given the city the highest average per capita income of any city in Brazil, but the profits do not reach most of the city's inhabitants. Thirty-five percent live in shanty towns like Vila Parisi with no social services."[1]

Cubatao may be the world's worst instance of industrial pollution, but too many other sites offer similar statistics and health hazards to account it utterly bizarre. In the United States the chemical pollution recorded around Niagara Falls, especially the toxic wastes deposited in Love Canal by the Hooker Chemical Company, provides a case study all too similar. We do not know the full implications of exposure to toxic wastes, any more than we know the full implications of exposure to nuclear radiation, but all indications are that it is very detrimental.

For example, the Japanese experience at Minamata Bay, where the methyl mercury discharged from a local chemical plant entered the fish, suggests that chemical pollution can cause severe brain and nerve damage. At least, those who ate the fish of Minamata Bay suffered such damage in completely abnormal numbers. The death of thousands of lakes in the Adirondack region of New York and the Canadian province of Ontario from the acid rain that industries in those regions have been producing is evidence that chemical pollution can be similarly lethal to animal and vegetative life.

Assuming that Christian believers, or humanists of any stripe, feel an obligation to promote life and oppose death, one has to regard today's ecological problems as a matter deeply religious and humanistic. Therefore, I think we ought to place ecology high on tomorrow's theological agenda.

The Place of Theology

Were we to place ecology high on tomorrow's theological agenda, we would significantly alter many Christian theologians' current outlook. By and large, Roman Catholic and Eastern Orthodox theologians have paid ecology little heed. Some Protestant theologians have done yeoman work, especially those influenced by the process thought of Alfred North Whitehead, but much mainline Protestant theology still rumbles along with little advertence to ecology, and almost all fundamentalist theology greets environmental issues with a crashing silence. The recent anthropocentricity of all the Christian traditions has made them slow to appreciate the religious attitudes underlying the energy and pollution crises.

A few examples may illustrate this assessment of recent Christian theology. Pope John Paul II's third encyclical, *Laborem Exercens,* is an analysis of current-day labor and economics sure to gladden the hearts of all seeking a more

5

humane working life. The Pope stresses the primacy of labor over capital, the ways work should serve people rather than profits, and the rights of laborers to band together and defend humane ends. On the other hand, he undergirds this humane labor theory with a reading of Scripture, especially of Genesis 1:28, that stresses human beings' commission to "subdue" the earth in a way bound to make ecologists shudder. As though unaware of the past decade's discussions of the place of Christian anthropocentrism in the rape of the earth, or of the need to establish rights for nature to oppose such rape, or of the many-sided problem of establishing a spirituality more respectful of nature, the Pope almost makes forcing nature to productivity the measure of human grandeur. Very little in his encyclical defends nature, or us human beings who are part and parcel of nature's ecosystems, from future pollution or despoiliation.

Pope John Paul II's encyclical but repeats his predecessors' neglect of nature,[2] and that of his brother bishops even in such otherwise advanced places as Latin America.[3] General surveys of Eastern Orthodox theology and Church life are similarly silent about ecological or environmental values.[4] Joseph Sittler and John Cobb are Protestant theologians who have long championed ecological values,[5] but lately their stream of influence seems submerged by the likes of Jerry Falwell and James Watt,[6] whose fundamentalist faith goes hand in glove with a capitalist economics stressing energy growth and development. Most recent Christian theology therefore has been part of the mind-set ecologists now challenge. It has been part of the problem, one of the ingredients that must change if environmental difficulties are to ease.

Specifically, ecologists now call upon Christian theologians to change the old image of "subdue the earth." The history of the various religions' attitudes toward nature shows that no tradition has been a simon-pure friend of the earth,[7] but it is Western technology that has set in motion the forces of modern pollution, and behind Western technology one finds an anthropocentrism that sees nature more exploitatively than Eastern systems do. Perhaps biblical religion need not

6

view nature so exploitatively. Perhaps it can expand its sense of stewardship into an equivalent of a Taoist reverence for nature's Way, a Buddhist reverence for nature's Dharma. Until it starts along this path, however, many ecologists will consider biblical religion a foe of the earth, a blind guide that has helped bring spaceship earth close to ditching.

This is not to say that all ecologists despise religious faith. Far from it. Many ecologists see clearly that faith, our basic attitude toward life and being, is crucial to how we work and play, how we treat our wealth of resources. If we could develop a faith more holistic, more peace-making, more feminist, more like ancient peoples' sense of Mother Earth's sacrality, we might offer the twenty-first century a new rationale to ease its interrelated crises of world hunger, nuclear arms buildup, and widespread pollution.

Central in the rise of these problems has been a lack of what Hindus call *ahimsa,* non-injury. Consequently, the religious attitude today's ecologists tend to propose stresses a sensitivity to the world's suffering peoples, a sensitivity to the aggressive psychology of the arms race, and a sensitivity to the wanton carelessness behind pollution.

Few works of art depict the spiritual pathos of our era as powerfully as Doris Lessing's *Canopus in Argos.* Let the following quotation from that work summarize the challenges Christian faith now faces (and do not miss the eucharistic symbolism): "She stands as she has done for millennia, cutting bread, setting out sliced vegetables on a plate, with a bottle of wine, and thinks that nothing in this meal is safe, that the poisons of their civilization are in every mouthful, and that they are about to fill their mouths with deaths of all kinds. In an instinctive gesture of safety, renewal, she hands a piece of bread to her child, but the gesture has lost its faith as she makes it, because of what she may be handing the child."[8]

Part One:

THE RECENT DIALOGUE
BETWEEN ECOLOGY AND RELIGION

The recent dialogue between ecology and religion involves an exchange of information and judgments on several fronts. In Chapter One we consider basic issues from natural science that frame the ecological crisis. Chapter Two takes us to technological and economic issues. In Chapter Three we study political and ethical issues. Chapter Four introduces religious issues, and so implies some of the deep questions of choice proper to dialectics. In each area we will only scratch the surface, but even that should give "ecology" greater significance.

Chapter One:
ISSUES FROM NATURAL SCIENCE

The Scientific Notion of Ecology
Before we go very far with our discussion, we should specify what "ecology" means and implies. G. Tyler Miller, Jr.'s marvelous text, *Living in the Environment*,[1] displays the scientific and sociological aspects of ecology in full detail. We can begin our specification by drawing from Miller's detail enough basic science to make clear ecology's enormous import.

Like the rest of natural science, ecology depends on some basic laws of matter and energy. Matter is anything that has mass and occupies space. Energy is the ability or capacity to do work or produce change by pushing or pulling some form of matter. Perhaps the most fundamental physical laws are the laws of the conservation of matter and energy. Materially, everything must go somewhere. In any ordinary physical or chemical change, matter is neither created nor destroyed but merely changed from one form to another. Thus everything we think we have thrown away or used up is still here with us in some form. For energy, the first law (of thermodynamics) is that in any ordinary physical or chemical process, energy is neither created nor destroyed but merely changed from one form to another. Thus the energy lost by a given system must equal the energy gained by that system's environment.

The second (thermodynamic) law concerning energy, however, points to a certain degradation. In any conversion of heat energy to useful work, some of the energy is always degraded to a more dispersed and less useful form. Thus, the *quality* of energy decreases in such conversions. The quantity remains the same, but the quality is degraded. As a result, a system of matter subject to energy conversions tends toward increasing randomness or disorder. For example, smoke from a smoke-stack and exhaust from an automobile spontaneously disperse to a more random or disordered state in the atmosphere. Pollutants dumped into a water-supply tend to disperse throughout that water-supply. The technical term for this tendency is *entropy*. Because of energy conversions, any system and its surroundings spontaneously tend toward increasing entropy.[2]

An immediate illation environmentalists make is that any society expecting to survive on a finite planet must become a low-entropy or sustainable society based on recycling—on reusing matter and reducing the use of energy. The alternative, a society of expanding growth, runs counter to the second law of thermodynamics. Today, as we use more energy to transform matter into products, and then shuffle these products around the environment, we are increasing the entropy, the disorder, of the environmental whole. The more we try to conquer the earth and subdue it, the greater stress we put on the environment.

Thus the ecological crisis comes down to simple blindness: We do not see how the world really works. Especially in the industrially advanced nations, we are living in blatant contradiction to the way the world really works, ignoring the basic laws of matter and energy. As Nicholas Georgescu-Roegen has put it, "Every time we produce a Cadillac we do it at the cost of decreasing the number of human lives in the future."[3]

The second energy law tells us that we are all interrelated and this interrelationship is what "ecology" has come primarily to denote. As *Webster's Third New International Dictionary* (unabridged) puts it, "ecology" is "a branch of science concerned with the interrelationship of organisms and their environment, especially as manifested by natural cycles and rhythms, community development and structure, interaction between different kinds of organisms, geographic distributions, and population alterations." For Miller, "ecology is a study of organisms in their home; it is a study of the structure and function of nature or of the organisms and groups of organisms found in nature and their interactions with one another and with their environment."[4]

A good example is the system, the whole, of a forest. There is sunlight falling through a canopy of leaves to reach shrubs and herbs growing at ground level. There are animals darting in and out, worms and insects crawling over fallen trunks and branches. There is water trickling from rocks and babbling by in narrow streams. Even the soil is busy with activity, as millions of bacteria and microorganisms ply their trades. The dynamic interactions among these and the other inhabitants of a forest are the exchanges of an *ecosystem*. Ecologists deal with organisms, populations, communities, ecosystems, and the whole eco (or bio) sphere. Their interest therefore spans from individual living things to the entire realm of life, the whole "system of interrelated ecosystems."

As its ideal, ecology pursues a complete understanding of the entire ecosphere. It wants to know all it can know, ideally all there is to know, about the realm of life. Inevitably this desire forces it to pay attention to the realm below life, filled with abiotic components, and the realms beyond earthly or physical life, such as the planets and the realm of thought (noosphere). Whatever affects the ecosphere is grist for the ecologist's mill. So the ecologist's hallmark is a concern for the interrelatedness of things, the constant changes, mutual influences, supports and dependencies that criss-cross the ecosphere. Climate, food, human population, energy, and pollution all come across the ecologist's desk. The seas and the deserts, the skies and the cities, all claim a place on her mental map. If the politics of a given society changes, for instance by the installation of a new Secretary of the Interior, the good ecologist goes on guard. He knows that new policies toward the land will alter all the land's relations, ultimately will touch the entire ecosphere.

The State of the Waters[5]

An important part of the ecosphere that the land and its human inhabitants touch is the waters, both those of the seas and those of the continents. Today the waters are in trouble. All but a few of the 246 water basins in the United States are somewhat polluted. The situation is similar in other countries, especially those that farm and do industrial business the way the United States does. Farming is prominent in any discussion of the inland waters, because topsoil erosion is now the worst cause of inland water pollution in the United States. Each year such erosion in our country would fill eighteen freight trains, each long enough to reach around the world. A third of the topsoil on United States croplands has eroded in the past two hundred years, and in less developed countries, where trees are cut down for firewood and marginal land is overcropped and overgrazed, the situation is perhaps twice as bad. Much of this soil erosion goes directly into inland waters, polluting them badly.

Agriculture is the major contributor, accounting for about three-fourths of the soil sediment entering the waters. Logging, mining, and construction are heavy contributors to the remaining fourth. Agricultural development can increase the natural rates of land erosion 4 to 9 times, careless construction can increase them 10 to 100 times, and uncontrolled strip mining can increase them 50 to 500 times. Unfortunately, ecologists have compiled these figures from experience. We have sufficiently polluted the waters and stripped the lands by careless agriculture, construction, and strip mining to have furnished scientists a great many instances on which to base their calculations.

However, soil erosion is far from being the only water pollutant. Human sewage, animal sewage, industrial wastes, mining wastes, urban storm runoff, the deicing of roads treated with salts, leaded gasoline, pesticides, the smelting of lead, fungicides, food-processing industries, electric power plants, tanker accidents, ordinary homes, and other sources all pour pollutants into the waters. Thus acids, metals, plastics, organic chemicals, oil, chlorine compounds, salts, and radioactive substances all pollute some of our waterways, frequently creating serious health hazards. In 1974 and 1975, scientists found at least 253 synthetic organic chemicals in the drinking water supplies of 80 major U.S. cities, at least 20 of which chemicals are possible carcinogens. Even the chlorine used by many water treatment systems has been called into question. In 1980 the Council on Environmental Quality warned of a higher risk of rectal, colon, and bladder cancers for people who drink chlorinated waters than for the rest of the U.S. population.

Our lakes are showing similar dangers and problems. Today perhaps one-third of the 100,000 medium to large U.S. lakes are endangered by accelerated eutrophication—plant nourishment speeded up by the addition of nitrates and phosphates from farming runoff and wastes, sewage treatment plants, animal feedlots, synthetic detergents, construction, mining, etc. In the 1960s Lake Erie seemed close to dying, because it was overnourished in this way. The massive doses of nitrates, phosphates, and various toxic chemicals it was receiving from major population centers in the U.S. and Canada were fouling its waters and killing its fish. Through intensive pollution controls, this trend was reversed. Most of Lake Erie's beaches have since been reopened and many of its sport fish have returned.

Groundwaters are also vulnerable to pollution. For example, as U.S. industries have struggled to comply with pollution laws, they have taken to injecting their liquid wastes directly into deep underground disposal wells. By 1979 there were about 500,000 such wells with injected fluids. In theory these wells are supposed to be safe, but cracks in their rock, the corrosion of their pipes, and underground pressures can all cause their infected waters to migrate. Even chemicals applied to the surface often seep down into the groundwaters. Scientists finally traced symptoms of arsenic poisoning found in a small Minnesota farming community in 1972 back to a massive application of an arsenic-based pesticide in 1934, when there had been a grasshopper infestation. It had taken 38 years, but the poison had finally percolated down to the groundwater that furnished the community its drinking water.

Thermal pollution is also a problem, and it is likely to increase as we develop more electric power plants. Such plants now account for more than 25% of all U.S. water use, and their discharges tend to heat the local waters above their natural temperatures. This especially endangers the ecologically vulnerable shorelines, where many fish spawn and raise their young. Behind thermal pollution lies the question of whether we need all the electricity we are building power plants to generate. The ecology of the land and the waters now includes the inreach of human energy, human technology, and human lifestyles.

Much the same holds for the oceans. Each year over 7 million tons of oil and petroleum are added to the oceans, mostly as a direct result of human energy needs. Indeed, more than half this amount comes from river and urban runoff and the routine intentional discharges of tankers as they clean their holds. While dramatic accidents such as the breakup of the Amoco Cadiz off the coast of France in 1978 (which released 67 million gallons of oil over 200 miles of coastline) get the headlines, business-as-usual makes the oceans more and more polluted. The 1980 draft of the U.N. Conference on the Law of the Sea was a ray of hope, but the Reagan administration quickly expressed a desire to renegotiate this draft.

The State of the Air[6]

What do such cities as Denver, Cleveland, Los Angeles, Louisville, New York, and Riverside, California have in common? All sit high on a 1977 Environmental Protection Agency list of 42 major U.S. cities ranked worst to best in terms of air pollution. In each city, the local troposphere (the zone extending 5 to 7 miles above the earth's surface, which contains about 95% of the air humans can breathe) housed such pollutants as carbon oxides, sulfur oxides, nitrogen oxides, hydrocarbons, photochemical oxidants, particulates, inorganic compounds, radioactive substances, heat, and noise. On the average, the troposphere now receives about 548,000 tons of air pollutants from the United States each day. That is about 4.8 pounds for each U.S. citizen. Since each person needs about 30 pounds of relatively pure air to breathe every day, our massive pollution of the troposphere bodes ill for our future health. In addition, it bodes ill for the future health of our crops, animals, and waterways. Indeed, acid rains and other air-borne toxic wastes are now settling over most parts of the globe.

Concerning human health, there are statistical signs that our current air pollution is part of a way of life in some ways considerably more lethal than what our grandparents enjoyed. In the early 1900s diseases of the heart and blood vessels accounted for about 20% of U.S. deaths. Today they account for more than 50%. There are many possible causes for this increase, but high among them stand the increased levels of carbon monoxide and sulfate particles that we inhale. The carbon monoxide comes mainly from automobile exhausts and cigarette smoking. Interacting 200 times more rapidly with oxygen-carrying hemoglobin than oxygen itself does, carbon monoxide ties up hemoglobin and deprives the body of oxygen. Thereby it seems to contribute to headaches, fatigue, impaired judgment, and a greater workload for the heart.

Although cigarette smoking is probably the major cause of chronic respiratory diseases, sulfur oxides, sulfuric acid, particulates, and nitrogen dioxide all aggravate bronchial asthma, bronchitis, and pulmonary emphysema. Indeed, while chronic bronchitis now afflicts one out of five American men between 40 and 60, urban non-smokers are three to four times more likely than rural non-smokers to develop lung cancer. Overall, however, emphysema is the fast-growing cause of death in the United States, killing about as many people as lung cancer and tuberculosis put together. In addition, about 1.5 million Americans (more than half of them under 65) cannot work or live normal lives because of emphysema. Manifestly, the air we breathe is dangerous to our health.

The most dangerous air pollutants are sulfur oxides and particulates. They come mainly from stationary fuel combustion (largely at fossil fuel power plants), but also from such industrial sources as pulp and paper mills, iron and steel mills, smelters, petroleum refineries, and chemical plants. Transportation also produces a significant share. Industrial smog, afflicting "grey air cities" such as London, Chicago, Baltimore,

Philadelphia, and Pittsburgh largely comes from the sulfur oxides and particulates produced by burning coal and oil for heating, manufacturing, and producing electric power. Such grey air is at its worst in the cold, wet winters of the cities listed. In an atmosphere of high humidity, the sulfur dioxide that the coal and oil wastes produce combines with water to produce sulfuric acid. If there is ammonia present it also produces ammonium sulfate. Together, sulfuric acid and ammonium sulfate apparently represent the greatest hazard to human health. Often rain washes them out of the atmosphere in a few days, but when it does not there can occur such disasters as afflicted London in 1952 (3,500–4,000 deaths) and 1956 (900 deaths), Donora, Pennsylvania in 1948 (20 deaths, 6,000 sick), and New York City in 1965 (400 deaths).

Photochemical smog, afflicting such "brown air cities" as Los Angeles, Denver, Salt Lake City, Sydney, Mexico City, and Buenos Aires, usually comes from a combination of a warm, dry climate and the nitric oxide produced by the internal combustion engine. In the atmosphere the nitric oxide becomes nitrogen dioxide, a yellowish brown gas with a pungent, choking odor. Ultra-violet radiation from sunlight causes nitric oxide and nitrogen dioxide to react with gaseous hydrocarbons (which come mainly from spilled or partially burned gasoline) to produce photochemical oxidants, and then photochemical smog. Such smog includes ozone and a number of compounds similar to tear gas.

Both grey smog and brown smog also contribute to acid rain. In places where sulfuric and nitric acid have formed in the atmosphere, the rain and snow may be as acidic as lemon juice. Winds can carry such acids long distances, making pollution sources in the United States major contributors to the acidification of Canadian lakes, and pollution sources in Great Britain and western Europe major contributors to acid rain falling on Sweden and Norway.

Acid rain eats into food crops, trees, materials, buildings and aquatic life. It is now a negative factor in the environments of the United States, Canada, western Europe, Scandinavia, Japan, and other industrialized areas. The United

States has planned to build 350 coal-burning power plants between 1979 and 1995. Under existing air pollution standards, this could add 10 to 15 percent more acid rain to the atmosphere. Already more than 300 lakes in the Adirondack Mountains are so acidified that they no longer contain fish, and Canadian scientists estimate that if their acid rain continues at present rates 48,000 Ontario lakes will be devoid of life by the year 2000. True, the exact causes of a given area's air pollution problems can be a matter of debate, as negotiations between the U.S. and Canada in 1981 over the acid rain falling across their border underscored. There is little room for debate about the general situation, however. Beyond doubt, recent policies concerning industrial discharges and automobile discharges have placed all the world's air in great peril.

The State of the Land[7]

The world's land is also in peril, from careless farming techniques, industrial wastes, and our continuing failure to heed the needs of the land's healthy ecosystems. An epitome of this peril are the amounts and kinds of solid waste we Americans alone foist upon the land. In 1978, each American produced an average of 20 tons of solid waste per year, 108 pounds per day. Such waste production has long been a problem, as anyone who watches a smelly procession of garbage trucks knows, but it has been increasing of late. In fact, the amount of solid waste we produce has been growing by 2 to 4 percent annually, which is 3 to 6 times the rate of our population growth.

The procession of garbage trucks notwithstanding, 56 percent of our solid waste comes from animal, crop, and forest wastes, 34 percent comes from mining wastes, 6 percent comes from industrial wastes, and 4 percent comes from municipal wastes. The proportions of the U.S. manure problem alone are staggering. The annual output of animal manure in the U.S. is equivalent to the wastes of a human population of 2 billion. At least half this manure is recycled by being spread on the land, but the rest is a potential hazard to surface and ground water, as well as a source of noxious odors, dust, and flies. Further, about half the 125 million steers who contribute to this huge amount of manure stand crowded together in feedlots holding 1000 or more cattle. For example, near Greeley, Colorado, close to 100,000 head of cattle stand on only 320 acres of land. When cattle and their manure occur in such concentrations, serious water pollution can be as close as a hard rain. Even without a hard rain, the gaseous ammonia from decomposing animal manure can produce excess nitrates in lakes and streams near the large feedlots.

More sobering than manure, however, are the hazardous and toxic wastes that occur in many industrial discharges. In 1980 some 750,000 producers in the U.S. created about 63 million tons of hazardous industrial wastes. As is true of the solid waste problem in general, this industrial production seems to be growing more rapidly than the general population, at a rate of about 3 percent a year. It includes a variety of toxic chemicals, such as acids, cyanides, pesticides, compounds of lead, mercury, arsenic, and cadmium, as well as radioactive materials. Some of these substances can cause cancers and others are suspected of causing miscarriages and stillbirths. The Environmental Protection Agency has estimated that only about 10 percent of our hazardous and toxic wastes is disposed of properly; 50 percent is simply dumped into unlined ponds, 29 percent goes into unsafe landfills, and 9 percent is burned, recycled, or dumped at sea (illegal since 1981). The rest goes into municipal landfills, sewers, wells, unused land, or is spread along the roadside by "midnight dumpers."

In 1980 the EPA estimated that there were 32,000 to 50,000 hazardous waste sites in the United States, perhaps 1,500 of which posed significant risks to human health and the environment. About 350 of these sites were judged so hazardous they were likened to chemical time bombs. The Love Canal episode allows us to color this phrase "chemical time bomb" all too garishly. Between 1947 and 1952, Hooker Chemicals and Plastics Corporation dumped over 21,000 tons of chemical wastes, most of it in steel drums, into an old canal, and then covered them with dirt. In 1953 Hooker sold the canal area to the Niagara Falls school board for $1, on the condition that the company would have no more responsibility for the state of the land. The town built an elementary school on the site and a housing project with 239 homes. Later 710 more homes were built nearby. In 1977 heavy rains turned the dumpsite to mud and its topsoil washed away. Chemicals from the badly corroded barrels then began oozing into nearby gardens and basements.

Health studies on residents of Love Canal later revealed an incidence of birth defects 3.5 times the normal rate, an incidence of miscarriages 2.5 times the normal rate, unusual numbers of nerve disorders, respiratory disorders, kidney disorders, and assorted cancers. Lawsuits and general fuss have clouded the questions of responsibility and liability, but none of the parties involved—Hooker, the local school board, the local and state governments, and the federal government—has emerged unscathed. All seem guilty of having underestimated the environmental impact of toxic wastes and, for economic or bureaucratic reasons, having blinded themselves to a potential disaster.

Analogously worrisome are the large amounts of cadmium, lead, mercury, and radioactive wastes now present in various parts of the environment. Cadmium, for instance, can accumulate in the human liver and kidneys, causing irreversible damage. At birth we have only about one-millionth of a gram of cadmium, but by age 50 the typical adult now has about 38,000 times this level. The accumulation is gradual but apparently relentless, helped by cadmium's long half-life (200 days), which means that it breaks down very slowly. Lead has been accumulating in the environment and human bodies in a similar way, so that we now treat about 15,000 children a year for lead poisoning. Perhaps 200 of them die and 5,000 of them suffer permanent damage. Methyl mercury can attack the central nervous system, the kidneys, the liver, the brain tissue, and cause birth defects, and we know that radioactive wastes can cause various cancers. Thus, in many places, the land has almost become an enemy.

The State of the Animals

Obviously enough, we share the earth's various environments with many different species of animals. Climatic and environmental changes influence these species just as they influence us humans. Indeed, all species of living things have to adapt to climatic change, competition with other species, natural disasters, and other forms of environmental change, so there is a sense in which extinction is a part of evolution itself, a given in the ecospheric range of possibilities. If there have been about 500 million species of plants and animals since life began on earth, as scientists estimate, only about 2 to 4 million exist today. Extinction therefore stands very high in the ecospheric range of possibilities.

Nonetheless, human interventions lately have so changed many species' environments that the rate of extinction has speeded up dramatically. By one estimate, human beings now destroy between seventy-five and one hundred thousand acres of animal habitat *every day*.[8] This makes plausible Miller's fear that we may exterminate 500,000 species of insects, plants, and animals between 1980 and 2000.[9] Such a number would represent 13 to 25 percent of all the world's present species, including such superstars as tigers, whales, and condors.

The prime cause of a species' endangerment usually is disturbances of its habitat, but commercial hunting, the introduction of competitive or predatory species, sport hunting, pest and predator control for the sake of livestock or crops, collection of specimens for pets or research, and pollution also can be factors. An especial problem nowadays is the elimination of tropical forests in Africa, Asia, and Latin America which house thousands of species.

The best hope for many endangered species is the enlightened policies of zoos that are cooperating to try to mate them in captivity. Although frequently such mating proves unsuccessful, and there are questions about how it changes a strain, it and efforts to reintroduce endangered species into suitable habitats have brought a ray of hope. However, one should not underestimate the problems this venture faces, especially in its efforts to reintroduce species into a natural habitat. For example, to place the 750 Siberian tigers currently in zoos in a suitable environment would require an area about four times the size of Yellowstone National Park.

Nor should one underestimate the complexity of the interactions among species, which makes all human interventions in the environment risky. Consider, for instance, the accidental introduction of the sea lamprey into the Great Lakes. The sea lamprey is a primitive, parasitic vertebrate with an eellike body and a round, sucking mouth. It attaches itself to fish, rips holes in their skin with its rasping tongue and sharp teeth, and then sucks out their blood and body fluids. Originally the sea lamprey ranged in saltwater off the Atlantic coast, from Labrador to Florida. It adapts to fresh water easily, however, and over the centuries it moved into the St. Lawrence River. The Niagara Falls kept it out of Lake Erie and the other Great Lakes until 1829, when the Welland Ship Canal gave it a way around the Falls. For a century the lamprey spread through the Great Lakes, thriving because they contained none of its natural enemies. When the Welland Canal was deepened in 1932, many more lampreys entered the Great Lakes. Between 1940 and 1960, the lamprey, along with overfishing and pollution, caused a 97 percent decrease in the whitefish, sturgeon, and trout fishing industries of the Great Lakes. After much testing, scientists found a poison that destroys lamprey larvae without harming other fish. By applying this poison to all lamprey-spawning tributaries of the Great Lakes in 1962, scientists cut the population by 80 percent and reestablished the Great Lakes' fishing industry.

American history contains even more spectacular stories of human intervention, among them the famous story of the decimation of the American bison or buffalo. In the middle 1880s perhaps 60 million bison roamed the North American prairies. As the railroads spread West they employed professional hunters to kill bison for food, and later hunters killed millions for their hides. When the U.S. government undertook to subdue the Plains Indians, it endorsed a policy of killing off the Indians' food supply, the bison. Between 1870 and 1875 at least 2.5 million bison were slaughtered each year. Only a few bison have remained through this century, sheltered in captivity.

Whales might tell an analogous story. In 1900 there were perhaps 4.4 million whales swimming the oceans, in 11 species considered worth hunting. Today all but three of these species (sperm, minke, and sei) are endangered, and only about 1.1 million huntable whales remain. That means that in less than a century almost three-quarters of the world's huntable whales have disappeared, including many of our largest animals, the blue whales.

Granted all the world's pressing problems, it is hard to make a case for placing the preservation of endangered animal species high on the list of international priorities. But ecologists see this problem as part and parcel of a gigantic collective threat to the biosphere. We do not know enough about the interactions among the animals to be able to eliminate some species with surety that others, including ourselves, will not suffer unexpected consequences. "Nobody could have guessed that armadillos would become useful in the study of leprosy, as they have. Nobody could have foretold that capybaras harbor an anti-leukemic agent in their blood. There are strong theoretical grounds for the fear that the loss of species may have very serious consequences for man, but most of these grounds either cannot be proved or offer unconvincing alternatives to exploitation."[10] Thus it is only a new ecological ethic, extending our prohibitions against human killing and destructiveness to sub-human species, that would offer the animals a radical hope for a better state.

Chapter Two:
TECHNOLOGICAL AND
ECONOMIC ISSUES

Nuclear Power

While we await the development of a new ecological ethic, many of the changes in our milieu occur through a technology we seem almost unable to control. Jacques Ellul has been among the most eloquent analysts of the price we are paying for the dominance of technology in contemporary culture,[1] and for him an ecological ethic goes hand in hand with a stress on the transcendence of the biblical God (who alone offers a point "outside," from which to criticize the technological system). Ellul also spotlights the dangers of nuclear power, utilizing the freedom of his biblical faith to criticize the cynicism of officials who press ahead with nuclear development while admitting that problems such as disposing of radioactive waste may be insoluble: "Let me tell you of an experience that strikes me as dreadfully enlightening in its cynicism. I am rather well acquainted with the president of *Electricité de France* (the French national utilities company which is also responsible for the nuclear power plants). I was talking to him, discussing the dangers of nuclear plants point by point. Finally, in regard to two items in particular, he acknowledged that there were indeed some insoluble problems. And then he made the following extraordinary comment: 'After all, we have to leave some problems for our children to solve.' That is the cynical attitude of the technical expert who knows his limits; it reveals that our children are indeed going to have difficult problems."[2]

For environmentalists such as Hans Alfven and Amory

Lovins, these difficult problems have already begun. Lovins has been a major proponent of meeting our energy needs through conservation (and solar energy), both because of the waste he sees in current Western usage and because of conservation's salutary effects on the ecosphere. (Thus he has found the French decision to develop nuclear power plants an almost classic instance of cart-before-the-horse planning.)[3] Alfven focuses on two problems, nuclear arms and radioactive pollution, that may well have been the "two items in particular" that Ellul pressed with the president of *Electricité de France*. Technologically, countries that obtain nuclear reactors are halfway to a nuclear arms capacity, because byproducts of commercial nuclear energy production (e.g., plutonium) are raw materials for nuclear weapons. Concerning radioactive pollution Alfven says, "Guided by a few very competent biologists, [environmentalists] learned how radioactivity induces cancer and produces genetic damage, and they discovered that the methods to keep the radioactive substances isolated from the air, water, and soil might work in a technological paradise but are unlikely to work in the real world. Now an increasing number of environmentalists have the same knowledge as nuclear insiders. They can now judge nuclear energy without the unavoidable bias of those who have devoted a lifetime to the development of nuclear power or invested $100 billion in this development."[4]

As Helen Caldicott, working from a physician's viewpoint, has shown, radioactive waste is indeed a terribly frightening danger. This is especially true regarding plutonium: "Plutonium is one of the most carcinogenic substances known. Named after Pluto, god of the underworld, it is so toxic that less than one-millionth of a gram (an invisible particle) is a carcinogenic dose. One pound, if uniformly distributed, could hypothetically induce lung cancer in every person on earth. Found in nature only in a remote region of Africa—and in minute amounts—plutonium is produced in a nuclear reactor from U-238 in quantities of 400–500 pounds annually! This alpha-emitter has a half-life of 24,400 years and, once created, remains poisonous for at least half a million years."[5]

Glenn Seaborg, the discoverer of plutonium, has estimated that we shall have produced as much as 1.6 million pounds of it by the year 2000. That would mean that as much as 32,000 pounds would have dispersed through the soil, water, and atmosphere, because up to 2% of our plutonium escapes into the environment. Even were we to achieve storage stability 99.99 percent reliable (which we are far from having at present), 160 pounds would be released. Caldicott calculates that 160 pounds of plutonium is enough "cancer doses" for almost 15 times the world's present population. Nor is plutonium poisoning only a problem for the year 2000. In 1975 the National Center for Atmospheric Research in Boulder, Colorado estimated that we had already dispersed more than 5 metric tons of plutonium over the earth as a result of bomb-testing, satellite reentries and burnups, effluents from nuclear reprocessing plants, and various sorts of nuclear accidents.[6]

"Accidents" probably conjures above all the incident at Three Mile Island, outside Harrisburg, Pennsylvania, in 1979. It happened that I attended a lecture by Caldicott at that time, so in my mind she is forever linked with Three Mile Island. Whatever quarrel one may have with the figures she spews forth, as with the figures almost bound to swamp any ecological discussion, I challenge anyone to dispute the humane instincts, the core sanity, she manifests. Actually, the very instincts that took her to a career in pediatrics have now taken her to leadership in the anti-nuclear movement. As both a doctor and a mother, she is saying that until we are sure nuclear energy is safe, we are foolish to employ it.

Today such surety seems a long way off, which is one reason why the nuclear energy industry is on the skids. Combined with the escalating costs of building and maintaining nuclear power plants, public doubts about the safety of such installations are tolling the industry's death-knell. One can regret some of the temporary economic hardships this may work, but for long range human and ecological survival it seems a pure blessing.

Intermediate Technology

If nuclear power summons many of the worst-case scenarios that critics of technology feel they have to write, the "intermediate technology" conceived by E. F. Schumacher has excited some of ecologists' best-case scenarios. Integrated with Schumacher's concern for the world's poor, and with his concern for preserving the ecosphere, this intermediate or "appropriate" technology is a fine illustration of why the philosophy of "small is beautiful" invites across-the-board application. Let us first see it at work in a specific situation, and then connect it to broader ecological issues.

In his posthumous *Good Work*,[7] Schumacher offers a vivid example of his technological approach. The President of Zambia had asked him to come as an economic consultant. When he arrived, he found the President despondent: Zambia's five year economic plan, which the President had been promoting around the country, was a shambles. The plan seemed to apply only to the cities around Zambia's Copper Belt and to its capital, Lusaka. It neglected the rural areas completely. Especially, it neglected the rural areas' malnutrition, their "protein gap."

Actually, the country had embarked on a nutrition program to close this gap, summarized in the slogan, "One egg a day for every Zambian." And, indeed, the Zambian farmers were doing a commendable job of producing eggs. But the program had crashed in its marketing phase. For lack of egg trays, the farmers could not send their eggs to market. Schumacher found them close to tears, watching their piles of eggs rot on the floors of their storage sheds.

Plunging in to earn his consultant's pay, Schumacher proposed that the Zambians start making their own egg trays. If the supply from South Africa, Britain, and America had dried up, why not produce egg trays locally? When he started to attack this problem, he found that most of the world's egg trays were made by one multinational company. He made contact with the European branch of this company, and it responded quite positively: "No problem. We'll build a factory in Lusaka." But there was a problem. Zambia's market was too small. It required only about a million egg trays a year, and the smallest of the multinational's machines made a million egg trays a month. The only way the company could conceive coming on the scene was if Schumacher and his colleagues could organize an All-Africa Common Market for Egg Trays (and have roads built to support the trucks necessary to carry the trays, arrange for currency exchanges, etc., etc.). For the multinational company, conditioned to bigness, small plants were simply uneconomical.

Undaunted, Schumacher took himself to the Royal College of Art in London and within six weeks had in hand a perfect egg tray. It was more stable and protective than the multinational company's, and it needed no crating, only a bit of string. That solved half the problem. The second half, creating a mini-plant, was more difficult. For this Schumacher consulted the Engineering Department of the University of Reading. They went back to first principles, thinking small from the outset, and came up with a plant having only 2 percent of the capacity of the previously smallest plant, and requiring only 2 percent of the capital cost.

The reaction of the multinational company deserves Schumacher's own ironic prose: "They said, 'Well, you know, we want to remain the kings of egg trays—that is our ambition in life. We have agreed that the small scale requirements we cannot meet—couldn't we come to some agreement?' They said, below this line of size it's yours, above that, it's ours. And in return for the privilege that they can remain the kings of egg trays, and not be disturbed by the little princes like myself, they gave us access to some of their know-how at the most ticklish points in the works, namely the mould which forms the egg tray. A healthy cooperation has developed between the whale and the sardine."[8]

Apply this "thinking small" approach to dozens of other areas—organic farming, biogas plants for villages, midget tractors, etc.—and you have the genuis of Schumacher's "economics as if people mattered." During his years with the British Coal Board, he had a ringside seat at the energy crisis, and it convinced him that conservation and renewable resources are the only sane long-range emphases. During his years with the British Soil Association he became convinced of the advantages of small scale organic farming. His work with the Scott Bader Company gave Schumacher the experience of an industrial cooperative that aimed at integrating labor and capital, in the larger context of an efficient, humane, and ecologically sensitive economic theory. His years of consulting in third world countries gave him an internationalist's sense of the interrelatedness of the world's ecological and economic problems.

Again and again, Schumacher ran up against the problem of scale.[9] Most Western technology, and most Western economic thinking, simply did not fit the needs of smaller or developing countries. The advanced countries had become so massive that their companies often were inflexible, unable to adapt to less than massive markets or needs. Therefore the incursions of first world technicians into third world areas often proved malapropos, even when they were well-intentioned.

Intermediate or appropriate technology therefore is but a species of the larger solution, the more creative imagination, that our cluster of ecological questions seek. Developing a better sense of both interrelation and scale, we need to become more responsive technologically, politically, and economically. Specifically, we need to fashion more *appropriate* responses to different peoples' environmental and economic problems, meeting an ecosystem or a village where it really is, not where our giantism says it ought to be.

Non-Renewable Resources

To meet the natural world where it really is, and not where our giantism says it ought to be, ecologists say we have to apply another of Schumacher's virtues, common sense. It is mere common sense to realize that if we live in a finite world, with finite amounts of non-renewable resources (e.g., fossil fuels and minerals), and if we keep using these non-renewable resources, then we will eventually deplete them. The only question is how quickly we will deplete them, and that is simply a function of the rates at which we use them. Interesting as it may be to debate the precise amounts of our non-renewable resources, the more basic issue is their finitude, which assures that if we keep using them they will one day be gone. For Schumacher the basic calculations involved are so simple one can do them on the back of an envelope. Just divide your best estimate of a non-renewable resource's reserves by your best estimate of humanity's future rates of use and you will have a rough timetable of that resource's depletion.

This becomes more than academic when one considers that technological economies such as that of the U.S. are dependent on specific resources for their continuance. Some simple figures make the matter dramatic: every second the world uses 30,000 gallons of petroleum and the United States uses about 10,000 gallons.[10] Further, ". . . every man, woman, and child living in the United States requires forty thousand pounds of minerals a year, if the individual's proper share of public roads, buildings, and the like is included along with the family car. (The American automobile industry consumes twenty per cent of the steel and iron castings, sixty-eight per cent of the lead, thirty-three per cent of the zinc, eight to nine per cent of the copper and aluminum, sixty-five per cent of the rubber, and five per cent of the plastics used in the United States.) Americans, who make up five per cent of the world's population, have in recent years been consuming twenty-seven per cent of the world's production of materials."[11]

Although the United States is the most conspicuous consumer of the world's non-renewable resources, the increased consumption of other industrializing nations has actually reduced our percentage. In 1940, for example, we consumed forty-two percent of the world's consumable resources.[12] However, despite the fascination of American analysts with figures concerning the United States, the bigger question is the future of the entire global community. Because of the tendency of so many nations to want the sort of economy the United States and the other Northern nations have developed, that future is rather dark.

For example, if one charts the estimated reserves of a

31

number of minerals and ask when, at a 2.5% increase in consumption rates per year, we would reach the point at which 80% of the reserves of the mineral in question would be depleted, the timetable that emerges is quite sobering. For gold we reached 80% depletion in 1979, for mercury we would reach it in 1983, for silver in 1985, for zinc in 1990, for lead in 1992, for copper in 1997, for tungsten in 1999, for tin in 2004, for molybdenum in 2012, for manganese in 2020, for aluminum in 2022, for platinum in 2028, for nickel in 2032, for cobalt in 2036, for iron in 2060, and for chromium in 2080. Even were one to project a fivefold increase in all these reserves, we would still reach 80% depletion of iron in 2140, having previously reached it for all the other metals.[13] When one considers the economic readjustments that the depletion of these metals will imply, a scenario such as Robert Heilbroner's,[14] in which nations either go to war over resources or they become subject to totalitarian regimes for strict citizen control, becomes quite plausible.

Similar charts are available for petroleum and coal. The fair predictions are that we should reach 80% depletion of the world's petroleum reserves between 2015 and 2030, and 80% depletion of U.S. petroleum reserves between 1990 and 2015. Similar predictions for coal put world depletion of 80% at about 2275 and U.S. depletion of 80% at about 2360.[15]

Awash in these figures, one can so contract the future that 400 years seems an immense time-frame. However, if one steps back to consider the longer survival of the race, the massive fact is that present consumption rates of non-renewable resources, whatever the world's funds of those resources should prove to be, imperil our race's surviving to the end of the third millennium after Christ. When one adds the population increases that are possible, the chaotic effects of increased entropy, and further damages to the environment, the future approaches the completely unmanageable. Just as the "greenhouse effect" of our heating the atmosphere may bring such massive changes as the melting of much polar ice and the consequent flooding of much coastal land, and the pollution of the atmosphere may destroy our shield against the sun's ultraviolet rays, many other effects of our consumptive lifestyle may bring lethal dangers. World hunger, competition for energy sources, genetic engineering, and radioactive wastes also likely will increase the political and military burdens already bending our psyches low.

In whole or part, figures and reflections like these are a major source of ecologists' convictions that we must decrease our dependence on non-renewable resources, become more conserving of the non-renewable resources we will always need, and adopt a policy of handling nature more gently. Simple survival, common sense about those elementary figures on the back of the envelope, finally puts the technicians' spate of computer printouts to shame. The bottom line is brutally clear. Many of the earth's resources are finite. If we keep using them at present rates, they will soon run out.[16]

Renewable Resources[17]

What, then, are the prospects for finding renewable resources on which to base the world's future economies? By and large, most ecologists find the prospects quite good. Bracketing the question of food, which we shall take up in the next chapter, we can concentrate here on alternatives to the fossil fuels and minerals whose demise we sketched in the last section. (To complete that sketch, we can add that natural gas supplies likely will reach 80% depletion for the world between 2025 and 2060, and for the United States between 2015 and 2040. The fuels necessary for nuclear energy likely would be depleted around 2130.)

First on most environmentalists' list of preferred energy sources is conservation. By "conservation" they mean improving the efficiency of current energy systems, especially those of the automobile and the home. The advantages of conservation are that we could implement a significant program fairly quickly, that the technology for it is relatively simple and well developed, and that it saves money. In addition, conservation reduces the deleterious environmental impact of harsher alternatives, extends our useful supplies of non-renewable resources, produces a very high net energy yield, does not increase the buildup of heat in the atmosphere, and requires little significant change in our lifestyles. (This last point may be open to debate, both as a matter of fact and as a matter of desirability.) The disadvantages that ecologists note include conservation's requiring mandatory regulations or strong economic incentives, "since it is very hard to implement by preaching and voluntary action."[18] Conservation also requires people to calculate their costs over a lifetime rather than just in terms of initial outlay, for the initial costs of purchasing and installing conservation devices can be high.

After conservation come the renewable energy sources available in nature, especially water power, solar power, wind energy, biomass energies (burning wood or crop, food, and animal wastes). The advantages of water power (hydroelectricity) include its source (falling water) being free, its having relatively low operating and maintenance costs, its technology being well developed, its being operable automatically from remote locations, its being plentiful in areas near rivers that can be dammed, its having a moderate to high net useful energy yield, its having a long life (50 to 300 years), its having a low adverse environmental impact on air and only a moderately adverse impact on water, its not increasing heat buildup in the atmosphere, and there being many (presently abandoned) small plants that we could put back into operation fairly easily. The disadvantages of water power include its being available (on a large scale) only in selected areas, most rivers near large population centers already having been dammed, the dams necessary to the system tending to fill up with silt, its destroying land ecosystems behind its dams and altering those below its dams, its requiring moderate to high capital costs, the difficulty of using it to power vehicles, and its altering the aquatic ecology. Tidal energy and ocean thermal gradients are subspecies of water power that may prove important in the future, but at present they present more difficulties than hydroelectricity.

Solar energy has been widely touted, but its technology,

including that of the photovoltaic cell,[19] is still in transit. Nonetheless, solar energy already offers a supply of energy that is free and readily available. The technology for converting individual homes and water heaters to solar energy is fairly simple, available, and easy to install, and solar sources offer moderate to high net useful energy yield, have a low adverse environmental impact, are very safe, and do not increase heat buildup in the atmosphere. The disadvantages of solar energy are that its usefulness depends on the local climate and the energy efficiency of local buildings (how they are oriented and insulated). It is not available at night, so it entails storage and/or backup systems (from conventional sources), and its production and installation costs are at present moderately high. Finally, to date we cannot use solar energy effectively to power vehicles.

Wind energy is free and readily available on breezy days. Its technology is fairly well developed, it has a very low adverse environmental impact, it generates a moderate net useful energy yield, it does not increase heat buildup in the atmosphere, and it can be connected to currently existing electrical grids (so that one can sell local surpluses to utility companies). However, winds are too weak in many places, wind energy in general requires a conventional backup system or an expensive storage system, presently it requires moderately high capital costs, and it is difficult to use for powering vehicles.

Biomass systems require large allotments of land and they make a moderately to highly adverse impact on the environment, but their technology is well developed, they have a moderate net energy yield, and their development costs are moderate. Such derived fuels as synthetic natural gas, synthetic oil and alcohols, biofuels, urban wastes, and hydrogen gas also hold promise, but their economic or environmental costs presently are rather high.

Thus, the tendency of environmentalists is first to plump for conservation, and then to urge the technological improvements that would make solar, wind, and water resources economically attractive. Combined, conservation and natural renewable resources seem to project both the greatest ecological efficiency and the least ecological damage.

Steady-State Economics

When one starts to consider what sort of economic system best squares with the intermediate technology, conservation, and stress on renewable natural resources that ecologists favor, the likelihood is that one will come to favor a steady-state economics. Although some ecologists favor such designations as "dynamic steady-state," which stresses that "steady" does not mean inert, the basic contrast is between an economic outlook that thinks in terms of growth, assuming its necessity and desirability, and an outlook that seeks a relative balance, replacing resources as it uses them and aiming at a rather simple lifestyle. The steady-state approach also implies stabilizing populations, and one can integrate it with a goal of achieving greater distributive justice (i.e., diminishing the gaps between rich nations and poor, so that all the world's people have a relatively equal set of opportunities).

As an introduction to the steady-state philosophy, it may be well to indicate the potential proportions of the conservationist impact. We Americans now waste 85% to 90% of our energy (get only 15% to 10% of the output from our energy input that theoretically we could or should). Each year we waste more fossil fuels than two-thirds of the world uses. Essential uses now account for only about 8 percent of the electricity we need annually, and we already have enough power plants to produce the essential electricity we will need to the year 2005, or even 2025.[20] Were we to mount a significant conservation effort, developing truly efficient transportation systems and housing units, we likely could halve our energy consumption. Clearly, that would make maintaining a steady-state economy all the easier, for it would allow us considerable leeway in specifying what a spare, conserving, recycling lifestyle need entail.

Ecologically, the basic stimulus to a steady-state economics comes from the elementary physical laws we examined in the first chapter. The first and second laws of thermodynamics imply that our economics best harmonizes with nature when we try to recycle materials and minimize entropy. Herman E. Daly, a prominent steady-state economist, has focused this basic outlook on more specific targets, however. Speaking to the World Council of Churches' 1979 M.I.T. Conference on Faith, Science, and the Future, Daly claimed there are ecological and moral necessities for limiting our economic growth.[21]

This claim was not completely novel. Many of those who have studied the depletion of our non-renewable resources have come to such a position. What was novel was Daly's stress on renewable resources. In his view, the greatest danger in our present economies is the damage they are doing to our renewable resource systems. "A reduction in the sustainable yield capacity of a renewable resource system, such as forests, fisheries, grasslands, and croplands, is a far more serious matter than the depletion of a non-renewable resource. The latter is, after all, inevitable in the long run. The former is not inevitable (except in the astronomical long run). Any permanent reduction in renewable carrying capacity means fewer and/or less abundant lives will be lived in the future. This reduction should be minimized if we aspire to be good stewards of God's creation."[22]

Still, we must not neglect the connection between our destruction of renewable resources and the rates at which we are using non-renewable resources. First, depleting non-renewable resources at our present high rates causes dangerous pollution of the air and water, and so directly threatens our renewable resources. Second, the rapid use of non-renewable resources has allowed us to reach, and temporarily sustain, a combination of vast population and high per capita consumption that our renewable resources alone would not sustain. As our non-renewable resources run out, we will find ourselves even more greatly tempted to over-exploit our renewable resources base.

In part, we are running into a problem of arable land. Jorgen Randers and Donella Meadows have estimated the total of the world's arable land at about 3.2 billion hectares. At present productivity rates we need about 0.4 hectares to support each person. Even if we doubled present levels of productivity and held population steady, we would run out of land around 2050. If we quadrupled productivity we would only put the crisis off until 2075. Once again, then, ecological considerations converge on a steady-state economics: "Because our environment—the earth—is finite, growth of human population and industrialization cannot continue indefinitely. . . . In a limited world we cannot maximize everything for everyone."[23]

Already one can document declines in the per capita productivity rates of the four natural systems on which humankind has always lived. (Until industrialization, two hundred years ago, none of the systems was in trouble.) Specifically, forest productivity seems to have peaked in 1967, fisheries productivity to have peaked in 1970, grasslands productivity to have peaked for wool in 1960, for mutton in 1972, and for beef in 1976, and croplands productivity (cereals) to have peaked in 1976.[24] Since we only achieved these peaks with the aid of large fossil fuel subsidies to mechanization, as we further deplete our non-renewable resources the peaks will be more and more difficult to repeat.

As I have said before, the point is not a particular set of figures. The point is accommodating a large human population to a finite world with a finite fund of resources. Achieving a species of stasis and balance, rather than aiming for constantly grosser national products, is how most ecologists tend to read the imperatives of our present times.

Chapter Three:
POLITICAL AND ETHICAL ISSUES

World Hunger

Flashing in blood-red neon, world hunger is among the most garish signs of our times. As the world population climbs toward five billion, and human longevity continues to increase, the finitude of those hectares of arable land looms more and more ominously. Already famine stalks Central Africa and South Asia, targeting the lower fifth of humanity, whom Robert McNamara, head of the World Bank, has called the "absolute poor."

Today the absolute poor number about 900 million. Even if we consider only half of them severely undernourished, we already have a political and ethical issue of momentous proportions. As Diogo de Gaspar has put it: "Hunger is essentially a food problem, the solution of which will require both greater production and improved distribution of food. Governments can take immediate interim measures to complement and support the necessary long-term development efforts. Raising the food intake of the over 450 million severely undernourished to the level of their nutritional requirements would involve the equivalent of 40–60 million tons of wheat per year. This is no more than 3–5% of present world cereal consumption, or 10–15% of the cereals now being fed to livestock in developed countries."[1]

For reasons both laudable and blameworthy, many commentators lately have been stressing the need to bring the impoverished countries to local food sufficiency, rather than having them rely on the wealthier countries' aid. Certainly any lasting solution to the problem of world hunger would seem to depend on improving local self-sufficiencies, but the stubbornness with which the wealthy Northern nations cling to the current world economic system, in which much of their affluence depends on arrangements almost sure to keep the Southern nations poor, tilts the whole problem. That 10–15% of the cereals now being fed to the livestock of developed countries, for example, almost always could be replaced with grass. As Nicholas Georgescu-Roegen put the trade-off in terms of producing Cadillacs or protecting future human lives, we might put the trade-off in terms of enjoying marbled steak or drastically reducing the number of human beings severely undernourished.

But what about the technological advances that, a decade ago, agriculturalists were touting as the solution to world hunger? What about the "Green Revolution"? As Sudhir Sen, for years a director of the United Nations Development Program, recently has argued,[2] the problem with the Green Revolution is the political implications it carries. With many technological wonders now in place, the problems tend to be land reform, good food distribution, developing rural road systems, and the like. For lack of such complementary supports, the Green Revolution threatens to abort, and with it the dreams of self-sufficiency conceived a decade ago.

For example, the rates of agricultural production in the third world often have not kept pace with population growth. Fifteen third world countries had lower agricultural production in 1979 than they had had in 1970, and in 1981 twenty-nine were suffering acute food shortages. In Africa alone people had ten percent less food in 1981 than they had had ten years previously. Along with Africa's increased population, that decline explains much of the world's imminent starvation.

In 1981, estimates were that worldwide grain production might drop 6 million tons, leading to rising prices and the greater dependence of needy countries on external food sources. Specifically, experts estimated the 1981 import requirements of developing countries at 94 million tons of grain, so the big questions were where the developing countries would get this immense amount, and how they would pay for it. Wheat prices rose thirty percent in 1981 alone, and the developing nations already suffered a collective debt of over $360 billion. By the end of 1981 world grain stocks were likely to be only 14% of world consumption, which was the thinnest of safety nets.

For Sen, the food crisis has arisen from folly rather than cold-blooded exploitation: "The world food crisis is essentially a post-colonial and post-World War II phenomenon. It stems not from cold-blooded exploitation of people, but from a lopsided application of science; not from the folly of individual nations, but from the collective folly of mankind."[3] The "lopsided application of science" that Sen had in mind is the disparity between medical and food assistance: "Since the Second World War the developing countries have received, in one form or another, a great deal of assistance in health and tropical medicine, while tropical agriculture has suffered from chronic and cruel neglect. WHO has set up a spectacular record of achievements, virtually stamping out malaria (even though it threatens to reemerge in some pockets) and other arch-killers; it has far outshone FAO in performance. Bilateral programs, too, have made large contributions to that end. And the transnational corporations have spread the biomedical revolution far and wide with a dazzling array of wonder drugs and medical technologies. The result has been a rapid extension of life expectancies, leading to an explosive growth of population in the developing world at a time when its food production remained stagnant or lagged way behind."[4]

So while laboratory scientists have developed remarkable new food strains, such as dwarf plants that give 5 to 6 times the traditional grain yields, the inept application of these new discoveries to indigenous third world conditions, along with failures in land, road, and political reforms, has meant the frustration of the food production that might have been. A country such as India did use the new technology to triple its wheat production from 1971 to 1979, but from 1960 to 1980 India's population went from 439 million to 683 million. Moreover, today India's agriculture, like that of many other developing countries, is still plagued by absentee landlordism and dispirited sharecroppers-at-will. Thus, the world still awaits the full benefits of the Green Revolution.[5]

Population Control

World hunger and increased world population obviously go hand in hand, but ecologists, demographers, and ethicians differ in the nuances they place on this interrelationship. At first glance, the demographers have the most stunning figures. In 1800 world population was about 900 million. By 1900 it had risen to 1.6 billion, the largest jump in recorded history.[6] In 1980 it was about 4.6 billion, obviously having exploded at exponential rates. Indeed, in 1980 the population of China alone was more than the population of the whole world had been in 1800. Similarly, as the figures we cited for India's population increase from 1960 to 1980 indicated, in 20 years India alone produced as many new world citizens as it had taken the United States almost 400 years to produce (by immigration as well as domestic births).

Such a vast growth in world population has had many causes, and many more consequences. High among the causes has been the improvement of medical science. Prior to the first decline of high mortality rates (in Europe in the late seventeenth century), world population had been relatively stable. As Teresa Sullivan has summarized it: "Most of human existence has taken place under demographic conditions of high fertility and high mortality, with very little population growth. Crude birth and death rates were probably in the neighborhood of forty births and deaths per thousand population per year. (By comparison, the crude birth rate in the United States in 1974 was 14.9; the crude death rate was 9.2.) Because of the equilibrium of deaths and births, this is sometimes called the 'high equilibrium' situation. However, death rates were not constant; they fluctuated with famines and epidemics."[7]

One of the further consequences of the better health care that has boosted world population is the increased longevity of the average individual. Not only do we save more infants, we keep all our people living longer. But keeping all our people living longer means keeping all our people eating longer, consuming more resources, developing new problems (such as the one on which Sullivan's study focuses, the vastly longer time period during which today's spouses have to get along). Through most of human history, half the females did not live to age 15, while more than half the males were gone at that age. Female life expectancy for those who survived to age 15 was about 49.2 years, male expectancy about 47.6.[8] Today life expectancy is about 78 for women and 70 for men. That means each human person today is consuming, over a lifetime, much more than twice the resources his or her historical counterpart consumed.

Moreover, the world's population has not been growing uniformly, as the contrast between India and the United States suggests. In 1950 34% of the world's population lived in developed countries. In 1975 that figure was down to 29%, and in 2000 it probably will be about 22%. In the year 2000, therefore, the population in less developed regions is likely to be 78% of the global total.[9] Imagine just the *political* impact of the developed countries' continuing their present resource usage rates to a year 2000 in which more than three-quarters of the world's people are "less developed"! Here are some of the present usage rates: "It is quite clear that the minority, living in the developed parts of the world, at this stage consume about 75% of the world's resources. They control about 88% of the gross world product, 80% of world trade and investment, 93% of its industry and almost 100% of its scientific and technological research."[10]

Barbara Ward has translated some of these demographic patterns into agricultural terms, speaking of "the fundamental problem of effective rural development in the third world. In fifty-two of the eighty poorest developing lands, there is less than 1 hectare of arable land available for each rural inhabitant (Canada has 25 hectares, the United States 23). Take India, Pakistan, Bangladesh. The minimum economic holding for Indians and Pakistanis is held to be between 3 to 5 hectares. In Bangladesh it is about 2 hectares. But the land available for each peasant in India is less than 0.5 hectares. In Bangladesh it is as little as 0.2. Even if land were redistributed on the basis of minimum-sized viable holdings, there could remain over 25 million landless families. How can any reform based upon the small family farm on, say, Japanese lines deal with this flood, this deluge, of landless people? However effective the supporting services, however large the rise in productivity, will not the inexorable growth of people beyond available and viable land simply become steadily more catastrophic?"[11]

Mention of Japan calls to mind an agricultural situation in which small has been beautiful, careful harmony with local ecologies has been very effective. Ward's book, on the whole, offers many such signs for hope. But in cases like Bangladesh, excessively small land holdings, due to excessively large population groups, have produced a politico-economico-ecological nightmare.

Therefore, we probably ought to take descriptions such as the following, from Catholic moral theologian Bernard Häring, with more than a grain of caution: "The crisis environmentalists tend to dramatize the food crisis, the exhaustion of the earth's basic resources, depletion, pollution, environmental degradation. Convinced that the population growth, if it continues unabated, is a matter of humanity's survival or death, they consider even the most drastic means of manipulation and coercion to be allowable and even unavoidable. Their writings contain enormous exaggerations and unproven presuppositions, for instance about the food crisis."[12] No doubt many ecologists' figures are open to debate, and some ecologists do not have Häring's Christian (and German) sensitivities to coercion and manipulation. Further, Häring's later remarks about Western wastefulness are extremely apt. However, there is simply too much evidence of the interrelation of rapid population growth, world hunger, and environmental damage for me not to think that most ethicians should be "crisis environmentalists" (rather than touts for humans' [hypothetical] capacity to increase food production tenfold). Most ethicians should be in the forefront of the ecologists' coalition for population control, not back with the footdraggers.

The Rights of Nature

Despite my misgivings about certain aspects of Häring's ecological ethics, he stands out as one of the first Christian moral theologians to integrate ecological problems and viewpoints into his overall theology. Influenced considerably by E. F. Schumacher, Häring is eloquent on the need for spare living, stewardship over creation, and even gentleness toward nature. Indeed, he finally comes to speak of a "chastened, sober anthropocentrism": "With all our reverence for whatever God has created by his almighty Word, we cannot overlook the levels of Being, the grades of significance, and above all, the position of man in the universe. A chastened, sober anthropocentrism implies a consciousness of our belonging to the whole. In a certain sense we can say, 'We are members of one another,' also in view of the sub-human reality."[13] The first part of this statement is less than many confirmed ecologists would like, but the second part is more than most other Christian theologians have offered.

At some remove from traditional Christian theologies of nature, one finds strong attacks on all anthropocentrisms, even such moderated versions as Häring's. Thus Paul W. Taylor has argued that the denial of human superiority is "the single most important idea in establishing the justifiability of the attitude of respect for nature."[14] Perhaps it is worth following Taylor's line of thought a few paces, for his is but an explicit presentation of views that many naturalists hold implicitly.

First, Taylor asks why humans should consider themselves superior to other animals. Why should we account the capacities that we have, and that they lack, things that exalt us and diminish them? After all, they have capacities that we lack. Cheetahs are speedier, eagles have keener vision, monkeys are more agile. Why do we not take these talents as signs that animals are superior to human beings?

The usual answer is that such human characteristics as rational thought, aesthetic creativity, self-determination, and moral freedom are more valuable than animals' physical gifts. But this begs some important questions: Valuable to whom? Valuable on what grounds? After analyzing rather carefully some of the semantic and logical implications of these questions, Taylor turns to such fonts of Western anthropocentrism as the classical Greek, Cartesian, and Judeo-Christian systems of thought. If Christians are to know their (at least partial) enemy in these matters, they should attend to how Taylor sees their anthropocentrism: "A third major source of the idea of human superiority is the Judeo-Christian concept of the Great Chain of Being. Humans are superior to animals and plants because their Creator has given them a higher place on the chain. It begins with God at the top, and then moves to the angels, who are lower than God but higher than humans, then to humans, positioned between the angels and the beasts (partaking of the nature of both), and then on down to the lower levels occupied by non-human animals, plants, and finally inanimate objects. Humans, being 'made in God's image,' are inherently superior to animals and plants by virtue of their being closer (in their essential nature) to God. The metaphysical and epistemological difficulties with this conception of a hierarchy of entities are, in my mind, insuperable. Without entering into this matter here, I only point out that if we are unwilling to accept the metaphysics of traditional Judaism and Christianity, we are again left without good reasons for holding to the claim of inherent human superiority."[15]

We shall consider the sorts of religious issues involved in any adequate counter to Taylor in the next chapter. My own position is that ecology must be part of a total worldview responsive to the evidences for God, the wisdoms of Christ, and the need of all creation, but especially human beings, for salvation. Since I doubt that Taylor's worldview would satisfy me, or most other theists, on these points, my "biocentrism" will be different from his. But he mounts a salutary challenge to any lazy anthropocentrism, and he has on his side the immense ecological damage that Western anthropocentric pride has unleashed.

Often as an extension of their anti-anthropocentrism, a number of ecological ethicists have argued for the *rights* nature has to freedom from human ravishment. Thus Anthony Povilis has argued, against Richard Watson, that if we take into account the ecological and evolutionary relatedness of living things, we have a basis for assigning animals and nature true rights.[16] This could dovetail with the desire of some ecological lawyers to enact laws safeguarding at least parts of nature (e.g., wilderness areas) by right,[17] and it could draw on such ecological interpretations of the golden rule as Julian Huxley's, in which we are to treat nature, as well as other human beings, as we want to be treated ourselves.[18]

Clearly enough, many advocates of ecological values do not espouse a radical biocentrism such as Taylor's, do not enter the thickets of analytic philosophy as both Taylor and Povilis do, and would not spontaneously imagine redwood trees and whales as fit subjects for rights in either human codes or a religious golden rule. However, the perspectives of current evolutionary biology, current analytic philosophy, future environmental law, and future religion are all germane to the future ecological ethics we need, so each of these perspectives deserves a fair hearing. If any can contribute to honoring creation as we should, and preserving planetary life as we should, we ought to try to find ways to account it an ally rather than an enemy.

Policies for Future Generations

Just as "nature" is too uncompelling a concept for many of our contemporaries seriously to consider according it rights in ethics or law, so "posterity" is too uncompelling. In many cases, the generations beyond those of their children and grandchildren exert no influence on the lifestyles of our contemporaries. Robert L. Heilbroner has ruminated on this problem in a postscript to his revised *An Inquiry into the Human*

Prospect. The postscript bears the Archie Bunkerish title, "What Has Posterity Ever Done For Me?", and we can use Heilbroner's opening musings to focus this issue: "Will mankind survive? Who knows? The question I want to put is more searching: who cares? It is clear that most of us today do not care—or at least do not care enough. How many of us would be willing to give up some minor inconvenience—say, the use of aerosols—in the hope that this might extend the life of man on earth by a hundred years? Suppose we also knew with a high degree of certainty that humankind could not survive a thousand years unless we gave up our wasteful diet of meat, abandoned all pleasure driving, cut back on every use of energy that was not essential to the maintenance of a bare minimum. Would we care enough for posterity to pay the price of its survival?"[19]

Heilbroner doubts that we would care enough. We don't seem to have sufficiently vivid imaginations to act today on the basis of what the year 2083, let alone 3000, seems to require of us. Indeed, respected economists have asked, "What is so desirable about an indefinite continuation of the human species, religious convictions apart?" Likening the time of our human species within the earth's history to a fraction of the journey (8 miles) of a plane trip around the earth, they have in effect said, "We are so brief a flicker we do not matter."

Although Heilbroner can find no logical flaw in this reasoning, it offends his more-than-rational depths. Indeed, he has come to see this sort of "rationality" as a powerful enemy: ". . . I suspect that if there is cause to fear for man's survival it is because the calculus of logic and reason will be applied to problems where they have as little validity, even as little bearing, as the calculus of feeling or sentiment applied to the solution of a problem in Euclidean geometry."[20]

What, then, might make us care for posterity? Resurrecting a rumination of Adam Smith, in which the great "patron saint" of self-interest (a) opined that news of a fearful earthquake in China, killing millions, would at best move the average eighteenth century European superficially, (b) thought further that news that this same European would on the mor-

POLITICAL AND ETHICAL ISSUES

row lose his little finger would trouble him profoundly, but (c) argued that no person of humanity, given the choice, would not sacrifice his little finger in order to save the millions of victims of the Chinese earthquake, Heilbroner comes with Smith to the faculty of *conscience,* the "man within the breast."

Conscience is that most human part of us that finally insists we take responsibility for our choices. Would those economists who view the extinction of our species with such cool detachment themselves write the writ of execution? Held personally responsible, would they remain so impersonally aloof? Heilbroner doubts that they would. The practical issue, then, is rousing the forces of conscience or personal responsibility, making it clear that we do indeed hold much of the choice as to whether our kind endure another thousand years. Assuming that most of us feel an "unbearable anguish" in the role of humankind's executioner, we should muster either the forces of those "religious convictions" that the economist casually tossed aside, or such analogously primal energies as "the furious power of biogenetic force we see expressed in every living organism," to create a practical rationale that gives us a chance to escape Armageddon. If the tragic scenarios that the next few generations will have to contemplate can lead them seriously to imagine the losses in a universe void of humanity, then we may hope humanity will find the means to ensure that the universe always has a reflecting part, a noosphere.

In different ways, such fellow-champions of human survival as Helen Caldicott and Gabriel Nahas share Heilbroner's passion and hope. Caldicott opposes nuclear energy and nuclear armaments because they strike at the heart of the Hippocratic oath she took to heal and preserve human life. Nahas is disturbed by the analogous problem of genetic engineering, finding it an affront to both future human generations and the whole biosphere: "I will comment briefly on the question of recombinant DNA and genetic engineering, which has also been called 'genetic meddling.' I believe that we are dealing here with an ethical problem more fundamental than one in public health or corporate profit. The main question is whether we

49

have the right to put an additional fearful load on generations yet unborn. . . . The relationship between bacteria and higher forms of life is still poorly understood. They are in one form or another waging a constant warfare against each other. By blindly transforming this relationship we may be throwing a veil of uncertainty over the life of coming generations."[21]

Eloquently, Nahas goes on to compare the two immense and fateful scientific discoveries of his lifetime, the splitting of the atom and the understanding of DNA. Insofar as both invite a willful interference with the homeostasis of nature, both invite a fundamental betrayal of faith. Unless scientists stop playing God, and start listening to what God has to say about preserving creation and evolution in the future, they may violate their basic obligation to posterity: "For those who remain behind we should leave a creation which is not profoundly altered from its natural evolutionary course."[22]

The Place of Aesthetics

The final factor I want to consider, before moving to precisely religious issues, is what I call aesthetics. Many ecologists move by a certain "feel" for the way we ought to live, the way we ought to handle nature. Their convictions largely root in what Michael Polanyi has called "tacit" knowledge,[23] a general gestalt so deep and holistic we can never express but a portion of its full "argument." A link between this aesthetics and our prior considerations occurs in the title of a fine (and somewhat pioneering) collection of essays on ethics-religion-ecology entitled *Earth Might Be Fair*.[24] If all men are to be glad and wise, as the song from *Godspell* that gave rise to the title of this collection dares to hope, we shall have to provide our children a better treatment of the earth, a more loving concern for her beauty, than currently we are.

The aesthetic component has many different aspects. It surfaces in the concern of architects and city planners to build human habitats that go with nature rather than against it.[25] E. F. Schumacher displays it when he waxes eloquent about a "Buddhist Economics" that would promote simplicity, ele-

gance, and fine quality.[26] The millions drawn to "the environmentalist movement" by the waste of the Western cultures—
the ugly signs, ugly housing, disfigured landscapes, disfigured
skies—are people in aesthetic revolt. Millions more who doubt
the wisdom of nuclear energy production, feel the attractions
of steady-state economic theory, or abhor today's massive
abortion rates are in similar revolt. This is not to say their sole
motivation is a vision of beauty or a repulsion by ugliness. It is
not to say that most anti-abortionists speak in terms of ugliness and waste. It is simply to say that "ugliness" and "waste"
play a part, and that they have many levels or aspects.

For example, scientists tend to favor "elegant" solutions
rather than "messy." Part of the appeal of Karl Rahner's theology is its core elegance (the jaw-breaking prose of its surface
notwithstanding). Sensually, intellectually, and spiritually,
we all feel a certain pull toward beauty: simplicity of line,
splendor of form. Many of the things nature itself makes are
overpoweringly beautiful: sunsets and flowers, a cardinal in
flight and a baby clenching its fist. So Lewis Thomas, the ur-
bane cytologist, was taken out of himself by the beauty and vitality of otters and beavers he saw sporting in the Tucson
Zoo.[27] So Gerard Manley Hopkins expressed many ecologists'
prayer when he gave glory to God for dappled things, for beauty that is pied.

Moreover when, with Robert North, one contemplates
"the world that could be,"[28] this aesthetics plays an important
role. Driven by hope, we are erotic for a future in which all our
relations—to nature, society, the self, God, and Jesus—are
lovely, beautiful, as the utopian in us knows they "have" to be
somewhere, someplace (called "heaven"). It is hard to underestimate such hope, sure a "lure" from God.[29] The difference between "is" and "ought" is a large part of what makes all us
Sammys and Sallys run. It is a "window of vulnerability" (to
try to redeem a phrase from Reaganite militarism) our species
constantly is trying to close.

In the West, we have been told that all creation is in labor, groaning to close the window of vulnerability, to bring
forth a world more redolent of God, more worthy of the Logos

in whom all things hold together. Part of our ecological imperative is the angel's "Hurt not the earth, neither the sea, nor the trees" (Rev 7:3). A thousand other voices from our Western traditions urge us to hope for a beautiful future. A thousand other instincts attributable to the Holy Spirit say earth really might be fair, earth's people really might be wise, were we to follow the lure of God.

So described, Western aesthetics is rather struggling, significantly a matter of what the Greeks called an *agon*, a mortal combat. Eastern aesthetics, which traditionally has been even less separable from religion than that of the West, has been more quietistic, more persuaded that if one achieves union with the Tao beautiful works will follow effortlessly, "mindlessly," as they do in nature.[30] In significant poets such as Saigyo, the Buddhanature replaced the Tao, but physical nature remained the font and exemplar of perfection.[31] By simply being perfect as a rose, impeccable as a lotus, nature better displayed the "suchness" (tathata) of ultimate reality than conscious, divided, struggling human beings did.

Japanese aesthetics, which has both inspired and derived from Shinto and Buddhism (especially Zen), is unthinkable apart from this orientation to nature. The famous Zen temples of the Golden Pavilion, the Rock Garden, and the Moss Garden all celebrate the peace and oneness of nature. The human "cultivation" that makes these temples elegant is understated, always on the verge of being chastened by purists, who value the wilder nature of more ancient shrines such as Ise.[32] In a literary mode, the novels of Yasunari Kawabata show this deep hold nature has on cultivated Japanese, the inalienably "ecological" imprint of the Japanese character.[33] Bridging East and West, Huston Smith's "Tao Now: An Ecological Treatment"[34] has translated the Chinese Way for American scientists and naturalists.

Chapter Four:
RELIGIOUS ISSUES

Simplicity
The Tao and the Spirit of God incline their followers to simplicity, harmony, and integrity. Profligate as nature can seem, wanton as evolution, we can see their dead ends and plagues as but prunings of branches, that the vine of dynamic creation may bear more fruit. Today ecologists with a religious bent are looking at the future demands of dynamic creation, asking what tomorrow seems to demand when it reaches into today, and they are finding a call to prune our foolish, wasteful ways. In terms of a Buddhist economics, the call is to simplicity. In terms of the gospel, it is to Jesus' sort of poverty.

To be sure, we must understand "poverty" and "simplicity" aright. Gustavo Gutierrez and other liberation theologians are fierce in their insistence that material poverty, such as that which afflicts most citizens of the third world, is a curse, something hated by God. Insofar as material poverty stems from the injustice of a few rich people, it brings God to the side of the many "wretched of the earth," moves God to a "preferential option" on behalf of the poor.[1] Biblical poverty therefore has to be an interior virtue, a sense of one's complete dependence on God. It cannot be a tool by which the wealthy try to keep the impoverished in a traditional subservience. The same with simplicity. It must be childlike rather than childish, a species of maturity rather than a species of dimwittedness.

Bernard Häring has captured much of the spirit of such a simplicity in the chapter of his *Free and Faithful in Christ, Volume Three,* that deals with ecology: "Conversion to the liberating truth and to beauty requires a creative detachment that has little to do with the old Puritan austerity that looked only for one's own predestination. Capitalism which, according to Max Weber, grew under the auspices of Calvinist doctrine and a corresponding puritan ethics, has unfortunately disowned what was good in that austerity. The remedy does not lie in going back to the poisoned roots. What we need are new models of simplicity that typify the beatitudes, joy, fullness of life, social responsibility."[2]

If poverty and simplicity be understood in this sense, much of the antagonism between ecologists and those working for human liberation might fall away, as Paul Santmire urged some time ago.[3] Then Marie Augusta Neal's "socio-theology of letting go" might include both social and ecological goals in one whole giving over of possessiveness and domination.[4] The greed that keeps so many members of the Southern hemisphere poor is of a piece with the greed that pollutes the environment. The austerity that might give the poor a better ratio of the world's raw materials is of a piece with the austerity that might hasten the day of an economy of steady state.

The answer to those in the developing countries who decry steady-state goals as "reflections of the anxiety of a pampered minority that its way of life is being threatened"[5] is not to abandon ecological goals but to show, through sacrificial work for distributive justice, that a steady-state economics need not mean continuing the presently unjust distribution of the earth's goods. In his great work on distributive justice, John A. Ryan long ago anticipated not only the question of how to achieve a radical equality ("No one has the right to luxuries so long as anyone lacks necessities"), but also many of today's ecological questions. For him, "The only life worth living is that in which one's cherished wants are few, simple, and noble."[6] Ryan believed that the foundation for such a life was religious. The fact that few human beings have managed to achieve it or enjoy it without being religious argues that he was very right.

Granted, a simple life, attuned to nature, may be "religious" in ways not traditionally Christian. It may stress a return to old, rural patterns and virtues,[7] a return to an archaic reverence for springs and trees,[8] or a "pilgrimage" to an anchoritic site like Annie Dillard's Tinker Creek.[9] However, in all these cases it involves a commitment, an act of faith (in the rightness of simplicity, and the wrongness of pollution) much like that of the traditional religious hermits, prophets, ascetics, and ministerial heroes. As well, frequently the ascetic side of such a simple life is balanced by an aesthetic side, showing that simplicity and artfulness are allies more than enemies.

This is obvious in such an artistic advocate of simplicity as Thomas Merton. In his later years, as is well known, Merton journeyed to the East, in spirit even before in body. One of the fruits of that journey was his "translation" of portions of the *Chuang Tzu,* an ancient Taoist text much revered for its wit, paradox, and insights into nature's ways. For the *Chuang Tzu* it is better to drag one's tail in the mud like a turtle than to be one of the great men at the imperial court, eminent today and very likely fallen tomorrow. For the *Chuang Tzu* the true men of old "slept without dreams, woke without worries. Their food was plain. They breathed deep. True men breathe from their heels. Others breathe with their gullets, half-strangled. In dispute they heave up arguments like vomit. . . . The true men of old knew no lust for life, no dread of death. . . . They had no mind to fight Tao. . . . Minds clear, thoughts gone, brows clear, faces serene. Were they cool? Only as cool as autumn. Were they hot? No hotter than spring. All that came out of them came quiet, like the four seasons."[10]

That is the sort of simplicity, properly adapted to our more technological times, that the religions should consider conspiring to inculcate. That is the sort of spirituality the ecological movement most needs.

Feminism and the Goddess

"Fine," half my readership may say, "the true men of old were simple, poor in spirit, attuned to Tao. What about the true women of old?" It is a valid question, only lately come forth from a neglect likely due to what some feminists call "androcentrism"—male bias.[11] As more women enter the ranks of theology and religious studies, more studies on women's religiosity appear. The interesting thing, for our purposes, is that much of the current work by feminists, both historical and speculative, focuses on a Goddess, or a set of feminist values, closely identified with nature. Indeed, feminist historians often underscore this identification and feminist constructivists often develop it vigorously. In both cases, the ties between environmentalist values and feminist religious values tend to be very close.

For example, Carol Christ's *Diving Deep and Surfacing* stresses that women's mystical experience often takes the form of a vivid appreciation of the great powers of nature: "Simone de Beauvoir, a theorist of women's experience but not of mysticism, has noted that women often experience a transcendence in nature that is closed to them in society. 'As a member of society she enters upon adult life only in becoming a woman; she pays for her liberation by an abdication. Whereas among plants and animals she is a human being; she is freed at once from her family and from males.' . . . It should also be noted that traditional cultural associations of women with nature and the conventional limitation of their sphere to children, home, and garden also encourage women to be open to mystical experiences in nature. In almost all cultures, women's bodily experiences of menstruation, pregnancy, childbirth, and lactation, combined with their cultural roles of caring for children, the sick, the dying, and the dead, have led to the cultural association of women with the body and nature, and men with culture, the spirit, and transcendence."[12]

This association of women with nature has come in for considerable discussion in feminist anthropological circles,[13] and much of the discussion is germane to the religions of illiterate and traditional (pre-modern and pre-technological, in the Western senses of those words) societies. In such societies, how the two sexes relate to nature (for example, women functioning as gatherers and men as hunters) usually patterns with their religious ceremonies, religious initiations, etc. The theological interest of many feminists, though, seems not to be these ancient correlations but reworking divinity iteself as fe-male and nature-related. Of course, this work, which Naomi Goldenberg has called thealogy,[14] often draws on the ancient historical goddesses, many of whom were identified with natural forces.[15] But it also flows into a "new witchcraft" that is explicitly ecological, explicitly concerned with establishing the close ties between feminist values and environmentalist values.

This is clear in *The Spiral Dance,* a poetic work of feminist witchcraft by Starhawk, a young adept. Speaking of the Goddess, Starhawk says: "The Goddess is first of all earth, the dark, nurturing mother who brings forth all life. She is the power of fertility and generation; the womb, and also the receptive tomb, the power of death. All proceeds from Her; all returns to Her. . . . The celestial Goddess is seen as the moon, who is linked to women's monthly cycles of bleeding and fertil-ity. Woman is the earthly moon; the moon is the celestial egg, drifting in the sky womb, whose menstrual blood is the fertiliz-ing rain and the cool dew; who rules the tides of the oceans, the first womb of life on earth."[16]

How literally this, and many other aspects of the new witchcraft, are meant to be taken is hard to determine. Pat-ently, though, naturalist values bulk large. Elements of na-ture—rocks, flowers, fire, water—play an important part in coven rituals, and harmony with nature is a high coven goal. Nonetheless, not all feminists are attracted to the new witch-craft nor to the old Goddess. Many women who wish to retain an allegiance to Christianity or Judaism rather stress the an-drogynous character of God, the male–femaleness (or tran-scendence of sex, insofar as sex would be limiting) of ultimate reality. Does this mean a lesser commitment to ecology? By no means. Rather more traditional feminists regularly associate the dominance of women with the dominance of nature, and so link the liberation of women with a changed attitude toward nature. As a stereotype, "masculine" technology has looked upon nature as a field to subdue, while male-dominated poli-tics have wanted to keep women in a subordinate role. Greater equality between the sexes therefore also offers the chance for a more balanced view toward nature, a view less warlike and aggressive, more nurturing and careful.

Rosemary Ruether and Dorothy Dinnerstein are two prominent feminist theoreticians who have popularized this sort of linkage. Ruether, for example, has written: "Women must see that there can be no liberation for them and no solution to the ecological crisis within a society whose fundamental model of relationships continues to be one of domination. They must unite the demands of the women's movement with those of the ecological movement to envision a radical reshaping of the basic socioeconomic relations and the underlying values of this society. The concept of domination of nature has been based from the first on social domination between master and servant groups, starting with the basic relation between men and women."[17] Thus, whether divinity be a goddess or the biblical God, harmony and justice mean the coupling of feminism and ecology.

Religious Studies as Ecological

The coupling of religious studies and ecology is a relatively new entry on the methodological scene, but one that holds considerable promise. In the main, it seems to follow the lead of cultural anthropologists, who for some time have been intrigued by the systemic character of human interactions with the environment. Thus twenty years ago Clifford Geertz, one of today's most honored cultural anthropologists (who, incidentally, has shown the disparities between Islam in Indonesia and Islam in Morocco), argued for the careful application of biologists' sense of interrelatedness to anthropological comparisons of human societies. Were anthropologists to be exact enough, moving beyond such bromides as "habitat shapes culture," they might greatly enrich our understanding of cross-cultural similarities.

For example: ". . . noncultivating societies with essentially the same hunting technology (bow, spears, deadfalls) may differ in various ways as a result of the kind of animals which exist in their environment. If the main game animal exists in large herds, say bison or caribou, it is adaptive to engage in co-operative hunting on a fairly sizeable scale. . . . If, however, the game is of the sort which occurs in small scattered groups and does not migrate, it is better hunted piecemeal by small groups of men who know their immediate territory extremely well—large population concentrations being impossible at any rate. . . . Thus, the patrilineal-band—small-animal situation is found among the Bushmen, who live in a desert, the Negritos, who live in rain forests, and the Fuegians, who live on a cold, rainy littoral plain. These groups show similar social structural features despite this contrast in habitats, because their environments are similar in the important matter, for hunting peoples, of the type of game they contain."[18]

Not surprisingly, the first appropriations of this sort of ecology by religion scholars have been occurring among those who work with peoples more immersed in natural cycles than modern, urban Westerners are. Thus Ake Hultkrantz, one of the foremost scholars of American Indian culture, has for some time spoken of an "ecology of religion."[19] As with Geertz, the point is quite specific correlations between types of environment and types of behavior. As Bruce Lincoln understands Hultkrantz's ecology, "He argues that just as there are 'types of culture' commonly recognized by anthropology, such as desert nomad and arctic hunting, so also there are types of religion that are intimately related to and in fact formed by the culture type in which they are found. He is very specific on this point and avoids any notion of historical contact or evolution in his theories. The type of religion is in its essence timeless: in principle it should occur wherever ecological and technological conditions of a similar level and integration appear. His goal is to establish these types of religion and to describe their essential features, drawing comparisons between cultures that may have no geographical or historical relation to one another but whose ecologies are similar."[20]

Lincoln's own work has followed Hultkrantz's further suggestion that a people's means of subsistence is the most important feature for cross-cultural ecological comparisons. Comparing recent East African cultures with those of the

Indo-Iranians who stand behind the Rig-Veda and the Zend Avesta, Lincoln feels he has been able to move across more than three thousand years (and no evidences of cultural diffusion) to find religions that are quite similar because they root in a similar "ecology." In both cases, a major dependence on cattle shaped a society in terms of a complementarity and conflict between priests and warriors. In both cases, the religion at the center of the society swung between the sacral activity of the priests (sacrifice, largely of cattle) and the sacral activity of the warriors (cattle raiding). Creation myths, religious ceremonies, and many other portions of each culture's "worldview" show striking similarities, because of their similar immersions in the obtaining, consuming, and appreciation of cattle. If ever one wanted a stimulating display of the potential significance of any religion's "environment," Lincoln's study offers it.

We would have to take great care were we to try to work up analogues for our contemporary Western situation, but the general thesis that peoples interact with their natural environments systemically seems well worth testing. Focused rather precisely on such features of the urban ecology as desk work and skyscrapers, it might illumine the often rather vacuous descriptions of modern urban religion as primarily shaped by "secularization." It also might more clearly define the reputed differences between the Native American and the urban American resonances to the land.[21]

An ecological approach to other religious phenomena glimmers on the horizon. For instance, Robert L. Cohn's *The Shape of Sacred Space: Four Biblical Studies*[22] is not far from proposing a mutual, "systemic" relationship between Israel's land and Israel's faith, with specific reference to such features as wilderness and mountains. Similarly, Denise Lardner Carmody's *The Oldest God: Archaic Religion Yesterday and Today*[23] argues that nature has been humanity's first deity, and it suggests many of the different ways, rooted in their different environments, that peoples as diverse as prehistoric hunters, Egyptians, folk Buddhists, Christians, Muslims, and native Australians have reverenced this first deity. Neither study is precisely ecological in Geertz's methodological sense, but both indicate the movement of "mainline" scholarship in Geertz's direction.

Sacramentalism

From Christian tradition, what Häring calls a "dynamic sacramentalism" may be many future theologians' response to the ecological crisis.[24] Such a sacramentalism would contest the view that "creation" (in preference to nature) is merely matériel to be used at human beings' whim. Rather human beings should use creation so that God's presence to it is transparent, so that creation is revelatory. When Christians celebrate their faith with such natural elements as fire and water, oil and wax, they take a creation in labor for redemption into Christ's story of salvation. When they transform the grain of the fields and the fruit of the vine into the body and blood of Christ, they divinize creation.

It would be comforting to be able to report that liturgical theologians are well into the work of linking sacramentalism and ecology, but this does not seem to be the case. If the papers of the 1978, 1979, and 1980 annual meetings of the North American Academy of Liturgy are representative, ecological themes currently are at best only tangential to professional liturgists' consciousness. Thus Mary Collins' "Critical Questions for Liturgical Theology,"[25] while in no way a direct response to the ecological crisis, does talk about the "bread sign" of the eucharist and could be expanded to include the more naturalistic motifs of this sign. Joseph Keenan's "The Importance of the Creation Motif in a Eucharistic Prayer" does come close to an ecological sacramentalism when it stresses the Roman Catholic Eucharistic Prayer Four's "You, the one good, and font of life, have made all things so that you might fill your creatures with blessings and make many joyful in the brightness of your light."[26] As with Collins', Keenan's study is hardly cause for ecological joy, but it offers a glimmer of what the more symbolically sensitive work of current liturgists might become, were someone to remind them how the natural world is being ravished, take them for a hike in the mountains, or perform any other of the corporal works of consciousness raising.

A slightly more useful reflection on natural symbols occurs in Raymond Vaillancourt's *Toward a Renewal of Sacramental Theology*. Admitting a partial validity in the charge that modern technology has desensitized our contemporaries' psyches, Vaillancourt yet argues that ". . . this supposed scientific and technological mentality of contemporary man does not go very deep. We need but push a little and we discover that behind a very pragmatic and utilitarian outlook there lies hidden a deeper attitude to reality that looks to what lies beyond earthly things and that grasps the symbolic meaning of reality. Here we are in continuity with the man of antiquity and of the Middle Ages who lived in a world of symbols. For the men of those times, water was not simply H_2O or water in terms of its physical components. It was certainly that, but the material reality was enriched with a whole range of symbolic meanings: water as life-giving power, as source of life, as agent of destruction. It is this symbolism, of course, that provides the basis for the sacramentality of baptism."[27]

These rather meager signs of hope need considerable bolstering before they will encourage any strong ecologist, but they remind us that the Christian doctrines of the Incarnation and Creation inevitably affirm the goodness of material creation, the goodness God himself affirmed when he gazed upon what he had wrought. My impression is that the doctrines of the Incarnation and Creation also keep a glimmer of ecological sensitivity alive in Eastern Orthodoxy. For example, Alexander Schmemann's *Introduction to Liturgical Theology* is formally weak on ecological sensitivity, but it expresses the continued commitment of Orthodoxy to a worship in which natural elements join in the praise of God. Were the Eastern Church to extend to nature its traditional sense of not merely being on pilgrimage but also already somewhat possessing its divine homeland, profound changes might come. For ". . . to the extent that the Church exists not only *in statu viae* but also *in statu patriae,* she embodies in worship her participation in God's Kingdom, gives up a glimpse of the mystery of the age to come, expresses her love to the Lord who dwells within her, and her communion with the Holy Spirit."[28]

For the Greek monks of Mount Athos, blending liturgical prayer and a spare existence in a lovely physical setting may inculcate more explicitly natural overtones.[29] In their environment the doctrine of the Pantokrator, the Logos as Lord of All, obviously extends to sparkling seas and jagged rocks, hardy trees and stunningly clear skies. If Eastern and Western monks keep talking together, so that the East impresses its deeper sense of the Logos' movement through creation on the West and the West explains the wide ramifications of the ecological crisis to the East, their dialogue may contribute significantly to a dynamic Christian sacramentalism. Until such a time, however, Western sacramentalists will have to do more with their biblical forebears' agricultural feasts, and with the nature mysticism of saints such as Francis of Assisi.[30]

Reverence for Life

Another helpful source for Christian sacramentalists who have at least a glimmer of the relevance of the ecological crisis would be non-Christian sacramentalism. For example, Raymond Panikkar has spoken favorably of Indian "iconolatry" (*karmamarga*).[31] When one recalls that many Indians, both Hindus and Jains, have joined a passionate use of icons to a doctrine of *ahimsa* (non-injury) extended, at least in principle, to all living things, one catches another glimpse of the rich promise a cross-cultural eco-dialogue holds out. Indeed, one wonders whether Western theoreticians of the life-cycle, who owe so much to Erik Erikson, couldn't find in such a cross-cultural eco-dialogue a stimulus to include "reverence for natural life" on the agenda of the mature personality, whom Erikson describes as mainly concerned with generativity and wisdom.

Generativity is fruitfulness of all sorts. It includes education as well as procreation, taking care of the world and society's present institutions as well as launching new personal or social ventures. Wisdom is the ability to love life in face of death. It is the main issue in the last of our epigenetic crises, the virtue we have to obtain if we are to live our last years well, give helpful example to the next generation, and die with integrity. It seems to me that Erikson's studies of Gandhi's generativity, which included *ahimsa* as well as *satyagraha* (truth-force), and Erikson's broad studies of wisdom, easily admit an ecological dimension.[32] The things for which mature people will have to care in the twenty-first century include, very prominently, the earth's ecosystems, as do the things wise people will have to be able to love in face of death.

No doubt, there will always be room for debate about what generativity and wisdom should entail in any given situation. One sees this, for example, in the controversies that have swirled around Garrett Hardin, a prominent ecologist who has proposed some of the grimmest future scenarios. Hardin has a penchant for vivid metaphors that drive his main contention home with a wallop. His main contention is that the limited carrying capacity of the earth (that finite number of arable hectares again, as well as the other limits to our global resources) should bring us to plan for a limited world population. The exponential growth in population recently has contributed to massive starvation in some places, and this has worked on Hardin's imagination to produce such vivid metaphors as "Lifeboat Ethics" and "Triage."

The first metaphor is clear enough: we are as though stranded in a lifeboat after a disaster, unable to carry all the passengers in danger of drowning. The second metaphor comes from French military medicine. In situations such as the battlefields of Vietnam, doctors often faced far more casualties than they had time, energy, or supplies to treat. Grim realism forced them to separate the casualties into three groups: those who probably would survive without medical attention, those who probably would die despite medical attention, and those for whom medical attention might make a crucial difference. They therefore concentrated on this last group.

In most general terms, Hardin's argument is that only self-help (increasing the number of those who can survive on their own) makes sense in view of the threats to the world's carrying capacity. We do no lasting good when we support systems that "ought" (in terms of natural laws) to go under. Despite a quarter century of significant humanitarian effort, the world situation today is worse than it was a quarter century ago: "A quarter of a century ago about a billion and a half people were malnourished. Now after 25 years of progress, two and a half billion are malnourished. Twenty-five years ago the poor of the world were increasing by one percent a year; now they are increasing typically by three percent a year. So things are getting worse faster."[33] Contrasting China, whom the West has helped very little with food and fuel, with India, whom the West has helped considerably, Hardin argues that benign neglect is the saner policy. China has done a much better job of becoming able to feed its 900 million plus citizens than India has done becoming able to feed its 600 million plus.

Hardin has certain facts on his side, but his hard-headedness about sacrificing (or allowing nature to sacrifice) some poor people goes down hard in traditional religious quarters, and for good reason. As Roger Shinn has pointed out in responding to Hardin's lifeboat ethics, the disproportionate consumption of the world's resources today means that lessened consumption by the affluent might save a great many lives among the poor, were our excess made over to their insufficiency: "Barry Commoner and many others have pointed out, as Hardin himself did, how much higher our rate of consumption is than most of the world. The figures he cited on food were about three to one, and energy about ten to one. My students from other parts of the world say, 'Such a little bit of retraction on your part could do so very much where we live.' "[34]

Hardin probably could accept this sort of transaction (even though he might not have Shinn's horror at the loss of human life) because spare living fits Hardin's general credo. The only aid he would consider anathema is that which ignores the inbuilt limits of the ecosphere. Thus he has lashed out at conceptions of God and progress that produce what he calls the dogmas of "Alladin's Lamp" (If we can dream of it, we can invent it) and "the Technological Imperative" (When we invent it, we are required to use it). Finally, Hardin's counter-religion seems to me eminently sane: "The religion called ecology—and let us admit it is a religion, a set of beliefs that bind us—also is built on two dogmas, the contradiction of the ones just given: (1) The Dogma of Limits: Not all things are possible (though death is!). (2) The Dogma of Temperance: Every 'shortage' of supply is equally a 'longage' of demand; and, since the world is limited, the only way to sanity ultimately lies in restraining demand."[35]

In a religious future, reverence for life should often be translated as restraining the demands that would injure nature's carrying capacity.

Part Two:

TOWARD A NEW CHRISTIAN
THEOLOGY OF NATURE

Having seen some of the major issues now being debated by ecologists and religionists, we turn to trying to sketch a new Christian theology of nature that might ease the current crisis. Chapter Five lays out some of the foundational attitudes proper to a converted Christian consciousness aware of today's ecological issues. Chapter Six deals with biblical doctrines germane to a contemporary theology of nature, and Chapter Seven deals with pertinent views from the later theological tradition. In Chapter Eight we attempt to systematize the most relevant doctrines of nature come down to us from the past, so that they make an elegant new package. Chapter Nine assumes the practical task of suggesting the major ethical implications of our new system, while Chapter Ten suggests some of the spiritual implications it seems to carry. In a brief Conclusion, we review the overall journey traveled in Parts One and Two and summarize our main convictions.

Chapter Five:
FOUNDATIONAL REFLECTIONS

Christian Conversion

A person begins to *speak* theologically, in contrast to *listening* to interpretations of data and debates about values in which religious issues may play, when she begins to express her conversion to a powerful, and perhaps new, religious center. The basic image at play in "conversion" is *turning*—shifting one's outlook, changing one's stance. Such turning can occur on various levels of consciousness, including the religious.

For example, we can shift our cognitional outlook, changing from a spontaneous belief that reality is a matter of what we see and hear to a hard-won conviction that the real is what passes muster as solidly verified. Again, we can shift our moral stance, changing from the easy position that goodness is a matter of what is pleasant to the more demanding position that goodness is what purifies the self and the community in truth and love. Third, we can become religiously converted, shifting from a horizon limited to the world of space and time to a horizon in which we try to love unrestrictedly, in response to a divine mystery we sense to be inexhaustible. Fourth, we can be religiously converted to Jesus, making him the privileged interpretation of divine Mystery, setting our hearts on Jesus' person and love.

There are numerous aspects to Christian conversion, and no single description of what it means to turn to Jesus, or to make Jesus the central value of one's life, is likely to be exhaustive.[1] For our purposes, the deep, foundational character of turning to Jesus is most pertinent. Whatever the initial motif a given theologian's conversion to Jesus may assume (for example, Jesus' character as a personal sign of God's forgiveness, Jesus' revelation of unimagined human possibilities, Jesus' intriguing goodness), when faith becomes reflective, and so starts to generate *theology* ("faith seeking understanding"), the shift in consciousness that conversion brings begins to mold the theologian's deepest sense of what "reality" can signify, what "God" or "human destiny" might mean. One has fallen in love with the unrestricted goodness at the center of Jesus, with the mysterious reality Jesus called "Father," and the Father's love has begun to rearrange one's previous perceptions.

Implied in this description of Christian conversion is a very hopeful view of human nature. If human beings can seriously turn toward realities such as Jesus' Father, can actually open themselves to the love of Jesus' Spirit, then human beings are not merely complicated forms of animality run by sophisticated systems of sensory stimuli and responses. Stimulated and responsive we are, but below or within the animality we share with chimps and leopards, deeper and more central, is an awareness of, an intelligent capacity for, a somewhat knowing vector toward a great deal more. As a matter of common experience, our minds press beyond the stimuli of food and sex, at times even seeking an explanation of nutrition and reproduction. Our imaginations design experiments to discern creativity and individuality that transcend what we can predict on the level of stimulus and response. Feelings for art and friendship drive us to unexpected sacrifices. And, above all, our hearts, our core selves, long to love, search painfully for a goodness worthy of total commitment.

To reflect on the fact of Christian conversion is therefore to muse one's way to the depths of the human condition, where many people claim to have found the presence of God. "God" is the holy mystery worthy of a total commitment. People who turn religiously to Jesus confess God, for they say that the holy mystery is present in Jesus with a unique beauty and power. Constructed to listen for a word, to seek a disclosure of God in the depths of ourselves or the depths of reality, we feel a gratuitous, telltale peace and joy when we hear God, when

God finds us. Saints and sages past and present, East and West, tell us that *nothing* is as powerful as this religious revelation. In their testimony, the revelation of God is attractive and fearsome as no finite, not clearly religious experience can be.

Most of us come closest to the awesome power of religious revelation through human love, when an unexpected force almost breaks our hearts with sweetness and pain. Romantic and parental loves, for example, can turn ordinary people into heroes, inspiring them to acts of creativity or endurance that their dossiers gave little reason to expect. These human loves are the best analogues to the saints' experiences of religious love, the source of the saints' heroic lives of self-denial, prayer, or service of their neighbors.[2]

Even if the individual theologian has not experienced a vivid religious conversion to Jesus, she should try to found her Christian theology on Christ. For unless it makes Jesus its bedrock, no Christian theology can hope to stand. With any lesser foundation, the tides of worldly opinion, personal confusion, or angry forces opposed to God will throw a theology off line, if not wash it away. The beginning, then, is Christian conversion.

The Sense of Grace

When we are religiously converted, the world becomes more gratuitous. No longer can we take any creature for granted. The mystery of God, the love of God that has seized our heart and restructured our consciousness, puts brackets around everything. Henceforth everything has another dimension, a facet of non-necessity, a message that it is a gift. To be sure, only very profound converts develop this sense of grace to the point that they find God in all things. For other believers, even those quite sincere and generous, the sense is a sometime thing, most likely to surface in times of intense prayer or unusual consolation. Other times the world can appear flat and factitious, a collection of uncomplicated signs rather than a treasury of icons and sacraments. Still, at the base of any genuine religious convert's awareness is an undertow of respect or reverence for the mystery of creation. We did not make the world. The world signifies a power and scheme beyond our scale.

The specifically Christian overtones to this sense of grace include the intuition that we have proven unworthy of the gift of creation and yet have not driven God off. By our dimness and disorder, we have frequently abused our fellow creatures, our fellow human beings most seriously of all. In a word, we are sinners, people who don't do the good they should do, people who do do the evil they should not do.

For example, the pollution of the ecosphere testifies to our sinfulness. The world has stood before us, ready to cooperate and serve, and we have turned much of the world into garbage. The injustice of society also testifies to our sinfulness. Fellow human beings have stood alongside us, asking to be treated as we would treat ourselves, and we have made wars and rapacious economies, slaveries and torture cells. Nonetheless, our sinfulness has not been the final word. Even when we have tried to ignore or defy God, God has not ignored or abandoned us. So a startling implication begins to dawn. God, the holy mystery, does not depend on our acknowledgement, our cooperation, our good behavior. God is holy and good because of God.

Any adequate theology of grace would want to place many nuances on this brief description, but most of the nuances germane to our project do not alter the description significantly. For instance, although it is true that nature sometimes has stood against human beings, threatening by tide or quake to wipe our species out, on the whole nature has been provident, as our having survived hundreds of thousands of years testifies eloquently. Indeed, today nature is so provident, or so amenable to human ingenuity, that we humans proliferate in staggering numbers. Nowadays the major threats to our survival do not come from nature. They come from human waywardness, human irrationality and greed.

Perhaps forseeing this, the traditional Christian theologies stressed God's kindness toward our waywardness. By his moral repair, his replacing our hearts of stone with hearts of flesh, God repeatedly has recreated the most dangerous of his species. Like a nursing mother, God has refused to forget the child of her bosom, no matter how evil the child became.

Understandably, then, one finds a strong sense of grace, especially of God's patience with human sin, in the mature work of all significant Christian theologians. Karl Rahner's *Foundations of Christian Faith,* for example, tends to make grace the central mystery, while Edward Schillebeeckx's *Christ* presents the New Testament convictions of grace in wonderous detail.[3] If Lucas Grollenberg's study of Jesus is correct, such mature works but verge on the central experience of Jesus himself.[4] The source of Jesus' great freedom to love, in Grollenberg's view, was his repose in God his Father. His Father made Jesus so full of trust that Jesus could drop most of the defenses the rest of us erect against fellow creatures or neighbors who can be threatening. Nothing could separate Jesus from the love of his Father, because the Father had riveted Jesus' spirit to himself, making their relationship Jesus' inmost definition, Jesus' deepest identity. When Jesus returned to himself, he tasted and saw the goodness of Israel's Lord. But that Lord no longer demanded awe and obedience. In the Kingdom that Jesus sensed was dawning, Israel's Lord wanted intimate love on the model of a parent and child. Though life slay him, yet would Jesus trust his Father, for his Father was light in whom there was no darkness at all, love in whom Jesus' acceptance was beyond question.

According to his capacity, the Christian convert reproduces these convictions of Jesus. According to her reflective gifts, the Christian theologian lays them down as her solid foundation. At the base of any mental edifice that is going to laud Jesus, one finds a bedrock sense of God's goodness, a bedrock conviction that God has treated us and our world kindly, lovingly, when he could have shown us wrath. We depend wholly on God for our being, and we have forfeited any moral rights we might have had by sinning. No matter. Even when our hearts have condemned us, God has been greater than our hearts, and God knows everything we need.

Nature in a Horizon of Grace

If Karl Rahner and Edward Schillebeeckx are two of the giants of the present generation of Roman Catholic theologians, Karl Barth and Paul Tillich were two of the giants of the past generation of Protestant theologians. Both Barth and Tillich said provocative things in line with our reflections on the sense of grace that Christian conversion tends to bring. Barth, for example, stressed the gratuity of human life: ". . . the blessing of life is a divine loan unmerited by man. It must always be regarded as a divine act of trust that man may live. And the basic ethical question in this respect is how man will respond to the trust shown him in the fact that he may do so. Will he recognise and appreciate the value of the gift? Will he realise that it is given him in order that he may use, enjoy and make it fruitful? Will he consider that he does not possess it for ever nor even for long, that used or unused it will melt in his hands and one day be finally past? Will he handle it as a treasure which does not even belong to him, of which he can dispose only according to the purpose of the One from whom he has it, and therefore not thoughtlessly nor arbitrarily, but remembering that he must finally give an account of his stewardship and use?"[5]

For Barth, then, life was something marvelous, not at all something to be taken for granted. We do not make life, so we ought to consider life a gift to be handled reverently, a trust to be used well. Barth mainly had in mind human life, but there is no reason not to extend his notion to all of creation. No less than ours, the lives of other creatures come into the world, and come into our use, gratuitously, as gifts of God. When we do not treat them as such, we abuse the divine generosity.

For Tillich, the divine generosity showed in a *continuous* creativity: "Since the time of Augustine, another interpretation of the preservation of the world is given. Preservation is continuous creativity, in that God out of eternity creates things and time together. Here is the only adequate understanding of preservation. It was accepted by the Reformers; it was powerfully expressed by Luther and radically worked out by Calvin, who added a warning against the deistic danger which he anticipated. This line of thought must be followed and made into a line of defense against the contemporary half-deistic, half-theistic way of conceiving God as a being alongside the world. God is essentially creative, and therefore he is creative in every moment of temporal existence, giving the power of being to everything that has being out of the creative ground of the divine life."[6]

More interested in philosophical questions than Barth, Tillich probed the ontology of creation and found that God must give beings their being continuously. In each moment we depend upon the only power sufficient to draw us from nothingness: the divine fullness of being. Like Barth, Tillich's main interest was human beings, but we can extend his line of thought to other creatures as well. Insofar as rocks, trees, elephants, and hummingbirds also depend upon the creative ground of the divine life, their every instant of existence, too, is due only to God's continuous creativity. In any of them, the observer with eyes to see can catch a glimpse of the divine power and beauty, the divine mystery of the world's origin and end.

The physical world therefore stretches before us not only as grist for our mills. In addition to being at our disposal, it stands before us as an invitation to pray. Since we did not make the world, and we cannot explain its existence, the world beckons us to praise the One who did make it, turn our spirits toward the One who can explain its existence. Nature is not a given in the positivist's sense: a brute fact with no further significance. Nature is a given in the religionist's sense: a gift from God's holy mystery, an expression of creative love. For the religionist, the person converted to the divine mystery as the supreme good, the world shines with further significances. Any creature may become a presence of God, a reminder of God's power or a promise of God's care. Certainly this was the assumption of most human beings through history, if recent archaic peoples have preserved anything of the early hunters' and gatherers' religion. American Indians, for example, felt that any creature might carry the power of the Great Spirit, might reveal the holy force that makes all of nature move.[7]

No doubt a theology founded in conversion to Jesus always has been able to look upon Jesus' God as the underived origin of the world, but only recently have the ecological implications of this view come to center stage. By failing to reverence the world God has created, we have disturbed many of nature's systems seriously. Not treating nature as a gift, not sensing God's continuous creation of our environment, we have lost vision and fouled the ground, the air, and the waters. Unhappy people that we are, what might rescue us from this lethal blindness? Nothing but a return to the light, a renewal of the convert's sense that everything exists only by God's doing, that nothing should be handled wantonly.

Sacramentalism

Eastern Orthodox Christianity has preserved the sense that nature is a manifestation of divinity better than Western Christianity. As David Tracy has shown in the case of Mircea Eliade, the Eastern Christian tradition has stayed closer to the archaic instinct that the cosmos is sacred, a manifestation of the ultimate holiness that makes anything be.[8] The result is what we might call a powerful sacramentalism—a powerful tendency to look upon creatures as holy signs. In the Eastern Orthodox liturgy, the pneumatic or spiritual power of the holy God fills bread and wine, water and oil, icons and vessels.[9] Like the incense that spreads to each corner of an Orthodox church, the spiritual power of the holy God spreads to each corner of the universe. The thrice-holy God is powerful and immortal, able to keep what he makes in being and life.

The Western branch of Christianity, especially the Protestant Western branch, has shied away from this sacramentalism. Seized by the force of the divine Word, it has wanted to empty the sanctuary of any created competition. With a sharp instinct for God's sovereignty, and a corresponding suspicion of idolatry, the Protestant genius has run toward proclamation. Like the biblical prophet, the Protestant reformer has felt compelled to proclaim a Word of God summoning human beings to pure worship and justice. Since impure worship usually is a form of idolatry, placing something limited where only the unlimited divinity ought to be, the summons to pure worship easily can encourage iconoclasm. Wanting to tear down symbols of fertility forces or worldly success that they thought obscured pure monotheism, some reformers also tore down the paintings, statuary, stained glass, and tapestries that had come to embellish Christian worship. In these reformers' view the only sacraments authorized by scripture were baptism and the eucharist, and, practically speaking, neither baptism nor the eucharist was as important as the bible or church preaching.

To this day, differences remain among the various Christian churches, but an ecumenical time finds the mainstream churches agreeing that scripture and the sacraments are not antagonistic but complementary. Each, in fact, partakes of both the manifestation mode of Christian faith and the proclamation mode. The scriptural word, for example, is not a univocal expression of God's mind or will but a richly symbolic, many-leveled expression. If recent scriptural studies have taught us anything, it is the diversity of genres and meanings both testaments contain.

On the other hand, it seems equally true to say that the sacraments proclaim God's will as much as they manifest God's presence. For Christian faith, neither baptism, nor the eucharist, nor any of the other sacraments that Roman Catholics and Eastern Orthodox celebrate is an amoral hierophany, a manifestation of divine power without an ethical demand. Rather all the Christian sacraments assume, strengthen, and intensify the demand of the biblical God for faith and justice. Those who are baptized into Christ die to sin and rise to a new

life of holiness. Those who eat the body of the Lord unworthi-
ly, not discerning its personal and social demands, eat it to
their spiritual peril. And so with the other Christian sacraments. Marriage, orders, anointing, penance, and confirma-
tion all proclaim God's Word of judgment and grace, at the
same time that they manifest the divine presence.

A principal utility of Christian sacramentalism for a contemporary theology of nature is its reminder that Christian
tradition has been as sensitive to manifesting signs as it has
been sensitive to the proclaiming words. If the modern West
became so preoccupied with proclaiming God's otherness that
it emptied the world of divine traces, and if this process of secularization contributed directly to our abuses of nature, then
we are wise to leave our current disorders and return to the
traditional balance between manifestation and proclamation.
Without denying the genuine Christian tradition of radical
monotheism and anti-idolatry, we should retrieve the neglected complementary tradition that the God of creation and incarnation comes to us through nature and our fellow human
beings. Historically speaking, Christian theology has affirmed
such sacramentalism whenever Gnostic or Manichean here-
tics threatened it by teaching that matter is evil. When they
anathematized this heretical teaching, orthodox Christians re-
peated the assertion of John that the Word became flesh, the
assertion of Genesis that God looked upon his creation and
saw that it was good, the Pauline assertion that all things hold
together in Christ.

A converted theology of nature would simply update this
sacramental tradition in face of today's ecological needs. Without denying that there are different levels of creation, it would
defend the rights of all creatures, both living and inanimate,
to respect and reverential treatment. Not blushing to learn
from other sacramental religions, it would emphasize the special holiness of places of striking beauty such as the Black
Hills of South Dakota or the Yosemite Valley of California,
agreeing that to destroy such places is a sacrilege. Beautiful
places are signs of God, manifestations of the divine nature
that give us grace.

Sins Against Nature

We have been portraying the converted Christian consciousness, in an effort to lay down the foundations of a new theology of nature. Thus far, we have stressed the sense of grace that conversion brings, the way that it tends to account nature a gift of God, and the sacramental overtones that it often finds nature's graciousness to carry. In this section we deal with insights reverse to these: the understanding of abuse that Christian conversion brings. When one turns to Jesus and starts to view the world as a gift of Jesus' Father's love, the sins of human beings against the world, our defilements of what we ought to treat reverently, stand out in bolder relief. Then our ecological depredations take on the lineaments of an egocentric denial of God. Were God in his heavens, we would not so pollute the skies. Were Mary still "star of the sea," we would not so pollute the waters. The ruin of nature and the denial of God go hand in hand, because both overexalt human beings. Long ago the bible described sin as missing the mark, failing to strike a mean. The accuracy of the bible's description is manifest today, when our imbalanced treatment of nature is bringing disaster down on our heads.

I will not rehearse the statistics assembled in Part One that support the charge of pending disaster. Our concern here is foundational; it is bedrock views of nature we want to examine. In many parts of the world, of course, people still live close to nature. Although this does not always make them conservationists, it tends to inculcate a deep respect for nature's powers and rhythms, a deep desire to go with nature's cycles rather than go against them. However poor, the peasant or farmer who works close to nature usually has a rootedness, a sense of place, that urban people, especially urban people of the highly mobile Northern technological societies, find hard to match.

To be sure, urban mobility offers many opportunities for growth, pleasure, and profit, but weighing these against the personal advantages of rootedness is not the most important calculus. The more important judgments we have to make today concern not our private advantages but the survival of our world as a whole. In making these judgments, we have to ask what lifestyles tend to beget responsibility for the earth, and what lifestyles encourage us to despoil the earth. Or, what lifestyles are consonant with faith's view that nature is God's gift, consonant with the convert's instinct that nature is sacramental? A short, negative answer is that lifestyles in which we simply use nature, usually at second hand, seldom make us friends of the earth. If a person seldom gives anything back to nature, seldom shows nature appreciation or care, he or she at least is vulnerable to ecological sin, probably is already in the midst of it. Why not develop the wilderness, build another power plant that will heat up the waters, build another coal plant that will smoke up the skies? If the dominant item on my agenda is an American lifestyle, with a ravenous appetite for energy, I am going to support nature's further attack.

Behind the despoilation of nature, then, one often finds sinful dispositions toward luxury. I want a luxurious lifestyle, rich in superfluities, and to obtain it I sanction nature's further pollution. Whether I realize it or not, my consumerist lifestyle, my enormous use of energy, says that this is my core disposition. More culpable even than such luxuriousness, however, is the pursuit of profit responsible for so much of our ecological devastation. The pursuit of pleasure tends to be petty and thoughtless, the ecological sinfulness of the weak. The pursuit of profit tends to be grand and calculated, the ecological sinfulness of the strong. Front and center among the strong stands the military-industrial complex against which President Eisenhower warned. Objectively, in terms of their policies' effects, the armed forces and development corporations are probably the biggest source of our sinful pursuit of an economy of ever-greater growth, an economy bound to devour more and more raw materials.

What does Jesus say about luxury and profit? Can a convert to Jesus make luxury and profit part of the Christian outlook? Jesus says that luxury, the easy life, is a deceit: "Enter by the narrow gate; for the gate is wide and the way is easy, that leads to destruction, and those who enter by it are many. For the gate is narrow and the way is hard, that leads to life, and those who find it are few." (Mt. 7:13–15) Concerning profit, in the sense of material wealth, Jesus is similarly harsh: "Truly, I say to you, it will be hard for a rich man to enter the kingdom of heaven. Again I tell you, it is easier for a camel to go through the eye of a needle than for a rich man to enter the kingdom of God." (Mt. 19:23–24)

In no way, therefore, can a convert to Jesus make luxury and profit part of the Christian outlook. At bottom, the egocentric, abusive attitudes that have led to our ecological crises diametrically oppose a Christian conversion. This does not mean the Christian convert must tell all rich people they are on the road to perdition. Evangelical strictures against harsh judgment restrain us from that. It does mean that simplicity, self-denial, and poverty are at the core of the Christian life. It does mean that many of the ecologists' instincts about what survival will demand in the future were anticipated long ago in Jesus' demands for simplicity.

Authenticity as Redemptive

The Christian convert believes that commitment to Jesus draws him forward to greater honesty and love. He believes that Christian faith is the inmost way to a life becoming more authentic—purer, deeper, more humane. Intellectually, morally, and religiously, genuine faith is a call to grow. One has to die to old, immature stages in order to be reborn with clearer insight, more balanced judgment, more generous responsibility, and more ardent love. How do ecology and nature figure in such a foundational scenario? If conversion means embarking on a journey of growth, what part is nature likely to play?

In the past, nature was likely to play several supporting roles. Frequently it provided retreats from harrying social affairs: quiet places in which to think about deeper things, regain the proper scale. Mesmerized by the sea, gazing at the mountains, or watching the sunrise in the desert, the religious person used natural stimuli to excite her praise of God, her repentance of previous egocentricity, her petition of God's powerful help. A second supporting role was provisional. Nature provided most human beings their food and shelter, so most human beings' religious interpretations of the struggle for subsistence and prosperity were deeply interwoven with natural memories, natural forces, or natural images.

Today, in the technological nations of the contemporary North, nature's roles are less immediate, though perhaps ultimately more decisive. Through the mediation of military scientists, nature now furnishes us lethal powers of self-destruction. Having let the nuclear genie out of the bottle, we live under a cloud of possible destruction. Standing on the verge of releasing a second, genetic genie, we wonder whether the skies will grow doubly dark. We now know enough about nature to garner doomsday might, yet we are not wise enough, or good enough, to be confident this might will make right. Today, then, nature first occasions our stark confrontation with the possible end of our species, a hard look at our moral disorder.

Nature's second contemporary role is economic. Natural materials such as petroleum and minerals focus the nations' current competition for wealth. Reflected in this competition are the many faces of human greed and injustice. What we do in polluting the skies or fouling the seas is of a piece with what we do through economic injustice. So the "manifestation" role of nature has turned quite grim. Eroded lands point to eroded bodies, and eroded bodies reveal an eroded sense of grace, an ecology and economy not resonating to the divine Spirit.

However, the converted Christian consciousness does not simply lament evil. In the paradigmatic story of Jesus, it sees the means to overcome evil with good. The growth of the convert in grace, the convert's progress in authenticity, is the minor drama of putting these means to the test. When the plot unfolds as faith expects, the struggle for authenticity is redemptive. Parts of the self once lost to sin are won back through penance and purgation. Spheres of darkness once indulged are illumined by the mind of Christ, the convert's slow assimilation of the gospel. If the convert's assimilation becomes fully mature, the presence of God becomes almost habitual. Eye does not see nor ear hear the full splendor of God, but the mystery of the beginning and the end dominates more and more of the Christian's attention, receives more and more of the Christian's love.

This redemption of the convert's personality affects all of his reality. It entails natural and social relations, as well as relations to the self and to God. Concerning nature, growth in Christian faith always has tended to deepen gratitude and sacramentalism. Today I suspect that authenticity regularly would take us to ecological issues, were we sensitized to see them.

For example, the gross disparities in human wealth that any mature conscience must face today are not purely a socioeconomic matter. Intrinsic to distributive justice is the issue of natural resources, of what consumption is sane and just. In global perspective, what converted theologian could stamp "authentic" on a consumerist lifestyle like the middle American? What converted theologian could encourage aspirations to the American fraction of the earth's goods? The only way to restore the earth to good health, and to care for all the earth's people, is to achieve common agreement that in the future "good life" will mean material sufficiency (but not luxury) and the preponderance of such spiritual pursuits as prayer, education, medicine, art, pure science, and social services. If this understanding of good life or authenticity takes hold, we may redeem nature from the effects of our recent ecological sins. If it does not take hold, we may expect horrible violence and suffering.

Chapter Six:
BIBLICAL DOCTRINES

The Law

Having sketched the foundations of a new Christian theology of nature, we turn to some of the traditional doctrines in which past converts to Jesus conceived their views of nature. First among these traditional doctrines are the teachings of the Christian scriptures, both Old Testament and New.

For the early followers of Jesus, the main scripture was the Hebrew Bible, and primary among the books of the Hebrew Bible were the Torah or Law—the Pentateuch or five books attributed to Moses. Of these Genesis and Deuteronomy probably are richest for our theme. Before turning to the law, however, it may be well to consider Israel's natural environment, for certainly the biblical authors' sense of nature was influenced by the land in which they lived. For example, Deuteronomy 8:7-9 depicts an idealized beauty and fecundity that had to have plausible roots: "For the Lord your God is bringing you into a good land, a land of brooks of water, of fountains and springs, flowing forth in valleys and hills, a land of wheat and barley, of vines and fig trees and pomegranates, a land of olive trees and honey, a land in which you will eat bread without scarcity, in which you will lack nothing, a land whose stones are iron, and out of whose hills you can dig copper."

Herbert May has summarized the climate of Palestine that shaped the promised land, emphasizing its variety: "The latitude of Palestine is roughly that of the state of Georgia. Because it is near the desert on the one hand and the Mediterranean on the other, because its main geographical features run N–S while the prevailing winds come from the N and NW, and because it varies so in elevation, Palestine has an incredible variety of climate and scenery. There are the occasional snows of winter in the highlands and the near-tropical climate of the Dead Sea; there are the pleasant rolling hills of Lower Galilee and the stark desert ridges of the Wilderness of Judea; there are the fertile plains of Esdraelon and the coastlands and the dry desert-steppes of the Negeb; there are rainless summers and wet and stormy winters."[1]

When the authors of the Pentateuch combined their experience of this environment with their understanding of Israel's providential history as a people covenanted to God and promised a special land, they both subordinated nature to the drama of human time and incorporated nature into this drama. Insofar as the first chapters of Genesis represent one of the classical meditations on these themes, their tensions epitomize the richness of Israel's instincts about creation. For example, two of the major interpreters of Genesis, Gerhard Von Rad and Claus Westermann, differ in their views of how universal the creation account originally was. Von Rad stresses the particularity of Israel's special covenant with God, while Westermann understands the early chapters as a general description of human nature. Brevard Childs has tried to resolve this difference by summarizing the canonical status of Genesis 1–11 as follows: "The canonical role of Gen. 1–11 testifies to the priority of creation. The divine relation to the world stems from God's initial creative purpose for the universe, not for Israel alone. Yet Israel's redemptive role in the reconciliation of the nations was purposed from the beginning and subsumed within the eschatological framework of the book."[2]

Other Old Testament scholars emphasize other aspects of Israel's sense of creation, but all of them underscore that the biblical authors saw the world in close linkage to God. Thus Samuel Terrien stresses the ties between the Genesis creation account and Israel's ceremonial Sabbath: "The ceremonial evocation of the 'genesis' of the universe (Gen. 1:1–2:4a) was told, not as a cosmogony destined to satisfy para-scientific curiosity, but as a proclamation of the holiness of the Sabbath within the creative act of God. The story of the genesis of the universe does not belong to didactic or epic literature. It constitutes the opening of a living *Torah*. Because it climactically leads to the divine pronouncement of the sacrality of time, it ushers in a new mode of presence. The creator may seem to be absent from history, but he is present in the cosmos and offers man a means of participating in divine creativity."[3]

On the other hand, Walter Brueggemann has emphasized that good Old Testament exegesis keeps space and time, nature and history, together: "In the Old Testament there is no timeless space but there is also no spaceless time. There is rather *storied place,* that is a place which has meaning because of the history lodged there."[4] In such key Pentateuchal passages as Exodus 16, Numbers 14, Deuteronomy 6 and Deuteronomy 8, the Israelite historians portrayed the promised land as both a gift from God and a temptation to self-sufficiency, both a task and a threat. So Israel's relations to the land became a major theme in the overall story of the people's progress and regress in faith. As physical as fertility rituals and kingship, the effects that possessing a land, a special place, worked in the Israelite consciousness were central to the unfolding of biblical faith.

The Prophets

Traditionally, the second major division of the Hebrew Bible is the writings of the prophets. Brueggemann shows that the prophets were especially sensitive to the way that the land of promise could become the land of problems. When Israelite leaders no longer looked upon the land as God's gift, no longer had a keen sense of stewardship, they brought the whole enterprise of the covenant and promise into question. Thus several passages in Jeremiah lament the king's failures, depicting nature's share in the great sorrow that Yahweh's rejection of the people will bring: "For this earth shall mourn and the heavens above be black; for I have spoken, I have purposed; I have not relented nor will I turn back." (4:28) "How long will the land mourn, and the grass of every field wither? For the wickedness of those who dwell in it the beasts and the birds are swept away. . . ." (12:4) "For a sound of wailing is heard from Zion: 'How we are ruined! We are utterly shamed, because we have left the land, because they have cast down our dwellings.' " (9:9) The exile that was to crash down upon the people meant the end of the golden time when the promise held: "The promise is voided. Jeremiah's images are of wilderness and drought, the terror of the land not sown (4:7, 23–26; 8:20–22; 9:10–11). The moment of the land, even four hundred years, has been lost. And the kings thought it could not happen."[5]

Although Jeremiah was the prophet who saw the fall of the Kingdom of Judah and the apparent end of the time of promise, predecessors of his such as Amos had anticipated the disaster, linking such signs of Israel's declining faith as not keeping the Sabbath, exploiting the land, and treating the poor unjustly to conclude that judgment was nigh: "Hear this, you who trample upon the needy, and bring the poor of the land to an end, saying, 'When will the new moon be over, that we may sell grain? and the sabbath, that we may offer wheat for sale, that we may make the ephah small and the shekel great, and deal deceitfully with false balances, that we may buy the poor for silver and the needy for a pair of sandals, and sell the refuse of the wheat?' " (8:4–6)

As Brueggemann shows, Hosea also linked the covenant's breakdown to natural imagery: "But covenant has to do with fidelity and betrayal, with embrace and abandonment. And that is the radical turn Hosea has discerned in the midst of his people. He utilizes fertility images to speak of *covenantal* realities. And he announces by that odd and effective combination of form and substance that the covenant is ended. It is voided, and with it the covenant gift, the land, is also forfeited. Covenant history, which had its fruition in the land, is now terminated. And the payoff is landlessness: '. . . lest I strip her naked and make her as the day she was born, and make her like a wilderness, and set her like a parched land, and slay her with thirst.' (2:3)"[6]

For Second Isaiah, who looked forward to a restoration of Israel, a return from exile and oppression to a new inheritance of the land, the old images of prosperity would be rejuvenated. In the future God would say, "In a time of favor I have answered you, in a day of salvation I have helped you; I have kept you and given you as a covenant to the people, to establish the land, to apportion the desolate heritages, saying to the prisoners, 'Come-forth,' to those who are in darkness, 'Appear.' They shall feed along the ways, on all bare heights shall be their pasture; they shall not hunger or thirst, neither scorching wind nor sun shall smite them, for he who has pity on them will lead them, and by springs of water will guide them." (49:8–11)

For Second Isaiah, the effort to trust in God's redemptive power, despite all oppressive evidences to the contrary, led to an insight into the contrast between the fragility of the whole created order, from grasses to kings, and the creative Word of God: "All flesh is grass, and all its beauty is like the flower of the field. The grass withers, the flower fades, when the breath of the Lord blows upon it; surely the people is grass. The grass withers, the flower fades; but the word of our God will stand for ever." (40:6–8) Eric Voegelin has amplified the power of Second Isaiah's faith in God's creative Word, imagining the context of the prophet's confession: "The fall of Jerusalem and the exile must have brought on a crisis of Yahwism in the sense that the power of empire seemed overwhelming and ultimate. The flesh apparently did not wither at all; Yahweh and Israel withered, while the gods and the people of Babylon prospered. It needed energetic reminders such as 51:12–13 that the powers of this world were mortal flesh, even if for the time being they seemed established forever."[7]

Like the historical theologians who composed the Pentateuch, the prophets associated nature with Israel's fortunes. The land was too central to the covenantal promise not to reflect Israel's overall fortunes in faith. Nonetheless, we note that neither the historians nor the prophets made much of the land or nature as a positive creation in its own right. By and large, their biblical perspective was ethnocentric. The land was a wonderful gift from God, and so should have been used well, but the land had few rights over-against its human stewards. Absent a modern understanding of the ecological relations that make nature so delicate, the biblical authors were not positioned to see that abuse of the land struck at the heart of a creative act larger in its purposes than Israel's prosperity.

The Writings

The third traditional division of the Hebrew Bible is the writings or wisdom literature. For our purposes, the Psalms and Job stand out. For example, a number of psalms praise God as the creator of the world, bringing nature into a hymn of praise. Psalm 8:3 is a familiar instance: "When I look at thy heavens, the work of thy fingers, the moon and the stars which thou hast established; what is man that thou art mindful of him, and the son of man that thou dost care for him?" The author not only praises God for the wonder of the heavens, he also uses this wonder to put human beings in proper perspective, striking a salutary blow against a false anthropocentrism.

Psalm 19:1 evokes a similar mood: "The heavens are telling the glory of God; and the firmament proclaims his handiwork." This is the *manifestation* motif we noted in the previous chapter, the deep instinct of faith to see nature as an expression of God's beauty and power. Psalm 104 praises the God who "coverest thyself with light as with a garment, who has stretched out the heavens like a tent, who has laid the beams of thy chambers on the waters, who makest the clouds thy chariot, who ridest on the wings of the wind, who makest the winds thy messengers, fire and flame thy ministers." (104:2–4)

Claus Westermann has admitted the power of the psalmists' appreciation of nature, without admitting that Hebrew faith gave nature any great rights. In fact, he finds in Psalm 8 a stress on human beings' special relationship to God: "God considers tiny humans worth a divine relationship, and shows this by letting them rule over the work of his hands—animals of all sorts. We moderns can hardly understand how lordship over the animals is a sign of honor bestowed upon us, for here we have an echo of a feeling for life from a very ancient age, an age for which the domestication of animals was humanity's highest achievement."[8]

Nonetheless, in reflecting on Psalm 19 Westermann almost equates natural creatures with human beings in that both oppose godless instincts that would ignore the mystery of creation: "In our time the creation psalms again receive important significance, because in the light of science and its results, as well as in our present stance toward nature, the deification of nature has no future (not even if it were to come in the most subtle form of Idealism). There remain only two alternatives: materialism or faith in the Creator. On the one hand, the stars, the atoms, and the earth are seen as only matter. Then we must be understood as coming from matter and consisting of matter. Or else the stars, sun, and earth are related to God just as we are; they are creatures. In that case the ultimate meaning of their living is the same as that of human beings: living to the praise of God's glory."[9] Psalm 104, perhaps the fullest of the creation psalms that manifest God's goodness, backs up Westermann's stress on praise.

Job also is replete with natural imagery and a respect for God's creativity, perhaps most famously in chapters 38–41. When God finally answers Job's accusations of injustice, speaking out of the whirlwind, his first argument is that he is the creator, Job is the creature, and never the twain shall share the same understanding: "Who is this that darkens counsel by words without knowledge? Gird up your loins like a man, I will question you, and you shall declare to me. Where were you when I laid the foundations of the earth? Tell me if you have understanding." (38:2–4) Of course Job does not have understanding of the world's creation, cannot discourse on the foundation of the earth, the moment when the morning stars sang together, or the time when God shut in the sea after it had burst forth from the womb. Therefore, God implies, Job should keep his mouth shut, his mind still. He should forget his legalistic theodicy, his ill-advised effort to justify God's ways to human beings.

Chapters 40 and 41 but repeat variations on this theme,

after Job has admitted his smallness. Only the one who has created Behemoth, Leviathan, and all the other wonders of creation knows the full scheme of things. For the author of Job, then, the splendors of nature can subserve human beings' struggles with evil.

Looking at the complexity of creation, we can see innumerable warrants to surrender ourselves into God's keeping. He who set the stars their courses easily can care for us. This care may take a form we don't like, but the heavens keep counseling us to trust. Marvin Pope has summarized Job's overall message in similar terms: "Viewed as a whole, the book presents profundities surpassing those that may be found in any of its parts. The issues raised are crucial for all men and the answers attempted are as good as have ever been offered. The hard facts of life cannot be ignored or denied. All worldly hopes vanish in time. The values men cherish, the little gods they worship—family, home, nation, race, sex, wealth, fame—all fade away. The one final reality appears to be the process by which things come into being, exist, and pass away. This ultimate Force, the Source and End of all things, is inexorable. Against it there is no defense. Any hope a man may put in anything other than this First and Last One is vain. There is nothing else that abides. This is God. He gives and takes away. From him we come and to him we return. Confidence in this One is the only value not subject to time."[10]

Insofar as it understood nature to point beyond passing human affairs to the God who alone is absolute, Israelite religion found nature a strong argument for God's goodness, even in times of deep suffering.

The Pauline Epistles

The Pauline epistles are the earliest documents we have from Christianity, and the first impression one receives from them is that Paul was not greatly interested in the land or physical nature. W. D. Davies makes this point, noting that Paul's own summary of Christian faith (1 Cor. 15:3–8) shows no interest in geography: "In this central recital there is no interest at all in geography. Paul is unconcerned with the location of the various appearances of the Risen Lord. They were a series of occurrences, unique in character, unrepeatable, and confined to a limited period, but not geographically located. No mention is made of Galilee, Jerusalem or, in the case of Paul himself, of Damascus."[11]

Davies relates Paul's unconcern with the land to the apostle's conviction that Christian salvation is pan-ethnic—that it has moved outside the covenantal line begun with Abraham and focused in the promised land. In other words, Paul's stress on personal faith in Christ led him to deemphasize the promised land: ". . . the logic of Paul's understanding of Abraham and his personalization of the promise 'in Christ' demanded the deterritorializing of the promise. Salvation was not now bound to the Jewish people centered in the land and living according to the Law: it was 'located' not in a place, but in persons in whom grace and faith had their writ. By personalizing the promise 'in Christ' Paul universalized it. For Paul, Christ had gathered up the promise into the singularity of his own person. In this way, 'the territory' promised was transformed into and fulfilled by the life 'in Christ.' All this is not made explicit, because Paul did not directly apply himself to the question of the land, but it is implied. In the Christological logic of Paul, the land, like the Law, particular and provisional, had become irrelevant."[12]

Nonetheless, Paul's deemphasis on land or nature stayed within the soteriological or salvationary horizon he had inherited from the Hebrew Bible. The land promised to Abraham and Moses, lamented over by the prophets, and epitomized in Jerusalem only fell away from the center of Paul's consciousness because the salvation that had occurred in Christ opened a whole new set of possibilities. Eventually the Greek philosophy that came into the Church through Paul's overtures to the Gentiles put forth a view of nature more detached from nature's practical or religious uses for human beings, but Paul's own thought was much more soteriological than ecological, much more concerned with the significance the land held (or did not hold) for salvation than with any value or intelligibility nature might have in a detached, scientific, non-anthropocentric outlook.

Regardless, certain Pauline texts have had great influence in the history of Christian faith's reflections on nature, and it will profit us to consider several of them here. Romans 1:18–23, for instance, has figured prominently in discussions of "natural theology" (whether one can reason to God from the evidences of the world): "For the wrath of God is revealed from heaven against all ungodliness and wickedness of men who by their wickedness suppress the truth. For what can be known about God is plain to them. Ever since the creation of the world his invisible nature, namely his eternal power and deity, has been clearly perceived in the things that have been made. So they are without excuse; for although they knew God they did not honor him as God or give thanks to him, but they became futile in their thinking and their senseless minds were darkened. Claiming to be wise, they became fools, and exchanged the glory of the immortal God for images resembling mortal man or birds or animals or reptiles."

Commenting on these verses Joseph Fitzmyer says, "Man, contemplating the created world and reflecting upon it, perceives through its multicolored facade the great 'Unseen' behind it—the omnipotence and divine character of its maker. Though essentially invisible, they are mirrored in the 'great works' (*poiemata*) produced by him (Acts 14:15–17)."[13] Edwin Cyril Blackman essentially agrees: "Behind the visible world is an invisible Creator. The universe points beyond itself to an Author whom human observers, if they really think, will recognize and reverence."[14] Properly viewed, then, nature points to God, shows God's existence and power.

Colossians 1:15–20, likely originally a hymn by a disciple of Paul, is a second noteworthy Pauline text: "He is the image of the invisible God, the first-born of all creation; for in him all things were created, in heaven and on earth, visible and invisible, whether thrones or dominions or principalities or authorities—all things were created through him and for him. He is before all things, and in him all things hold together. He is the head of the body, the church; he is the beginning, the firstborn from the dead, that in everything he might be preeminent. For in him all the fullness of God was pleased to dwell, and through him to reconcile to himself all things, whether on earth or in heaven, making peace by the blood of his cross."

Although the main thrust of this passage is soteriological, William Barclay suggests some strong cosmological implications: "Paul uses the strange phrase: 'In him all things hold together.' This means that not only is the Son the agent of creation in the beginning and the goal of creation in the end, but between the beginning and the end, during time as we know it, it is he who holds the world together. That is to say, all the laws by which this world is order and not chaos are an expression of the mind of the Son. The law of gravity and the rest, the laws by which the universe hangs together, are not only scientific laws but also divine."[15]

Certainly this is a view that Christian theology has little appropriated. The Logos doctrine (the Word of God as the principle of creation) has always held a prominent place, but we have little applied it to scientific laws, and not at all made it a basis for reverencing nature. Taken at face value, the text and Barclay's interpretation say that *everything* bears us a presence not only of God but specifically of the Son, the Logos, the person who became incarnate as Jesus and rose as the Christ. In addition to the cultural history of Jesus, there is a cosmic history, a sense in which evolution is a part of Christology. Teilhard de Chardin built his "Christogenesis" on Pauline texts such as this, but Teilhard continues to be judged an eccentric.

Barclay would not judge Teilhard an eccentric, as his further exegesis of Col. 1:15–23 shows: "We must note that Paul says that in Christ God was reconciling *all things* to himself. . . . The vision of Paul was a universe in which not only the people but the very things were redeemed. . . . This is God's world and it is a redeemed world, for in some amazing way God in Christ was reconciling the whole universe of men and living creatures and even inanimate things to himself."[16]

The Synoptic Gospels

Like Paul, the authors of the synoptic gospels thought that Christian salvation implied a movement away from Israel's preoccupation with a promised land. Mark 6:1–6, for example, shows Jesus finding no faith in his own country of Galilee: "He went away from there and came to his own country; and his disciples followed him. And on the sabbath he began to teach in the synagogue; and many who heard him were astonished saying, 'Where did this man get all this? What is the wisdom given to him? What mighty works are wrought by his hands! Is not this the carpenter, the son of Mary and brother of James and Joses and Judas and Simon, and are not his sisters here with us?' And they took offense at him. And Jesus said to them, 'A prophet is not without honor, except in his own country, and among his own kin, and in his own house.' And he could do no mighty work there, except that he laid his hands upon a few sick people and healed them. And he marveled because of their unbelief. And he went about among the villages teaching."

The message clearly is that Christian faith does not depend upon local conditions. If Jesus' own fellow-countrymen took offense at him and showed themselves faithless, then "land" in the sense of an ethnic locale had proven meaningless. There were no privileged places, no promised lands. The quality of an individual person's faith determined her or his salvation, not the place where she or he lived.

Both Mark and Matthew applied this conviction even to Jerusalem, which, with Judaism, they assumed had to be the center of the Messiah's destiny. Thus Mark 10:32ff. implies that Jesus had to die in Jerusalem, while Matthew 21:10 and 27:53 show that the author considered Jerusalem the center of the final drama. For Matthew that honor proved bitter, however, since Matthew thought that in rejecting Jesus the holy city had become the guilty city. The destruction of Jerusalem by the Romans in 70 C.E. (Common Era) probably supported the evangelist's opinion (expressed in the parable of the wedding feast [22:1ff.]) that God was bound to punish Jerusalem for having rejected Jesus' messiahship.

In Mark and Matthew, therefore, there is no Christian holy land. Is there, however, a holy land in Luke–Acts? Hans Conzelmann, for one, has suggested that Luke gave the land of Israel a significance quite like that it had had in Judaism. W. D. Davies disputes this thesis, but he admits that Luke shows a special interest in Jesus' journeys through the land, and that Luke is greatly concerned with Jerusalem. Still, Davies characterizes Luke's view of Jerusalem as an "honorable demotion" from the significance it held in Judaism.

One way Luke expresses this view is by separating Jerusalem from the Parousia, the Christian end-time of fulfillment. Jerusalem may have been the scene of the Christian beginning, but Luke 19:11 implies that it will not be the scene of the Christian fulfillment: "As they heard these things, he proceeded to tell them a parable, because he was near to Jerusalem, and because they supposed that the kingdom of God was to appear immediately." The parable Jesus then tells is Luke's version of the story of the talents, the conclusion of which is a stark rebuff to Jerusalem and the Jews: " 'But as for these enemies of mine, who did not want me to reign over them, bring them here and slay them before me.' " (19:27)[17]

A number of Jesus' parables employ natural symbolism, however, so we should not take Jesus' and the Synoptics' indifference to geographic locale as a general blindness to nature's significance. Pheme Perkins has considered several of these nature parables under the heading of "Parables of Growth," and she suggests that natural processes generally provided Jesus with analogies to the processes of human beings' religious growth.[18] In addition, Jesus drew metaphors from nature to make his teaching more vivid and pointed. For example, he used the weather we share in common to sharpen his exhortation that we love our enemies (Matthew 5:45). He pointed to the birds of the air and the flowers of the field to allay our anxieties about food and clothing (Matthew 6:25–33). Behind this tendence Perkins sees the instinct of the Hebrew Bible to assimilate the workings of God's word to a fruitful harvest. Thus Isaiah 55:10–11 has God eloquently proclaim: "For as the rain and the snow come down from heaven, and return not thither but water the earth, making it bring forth and sprout, giving seed to the sower and bread to the eater, so shall my word be that goes forth from my mouth; it shall not return to me empty, but it shall accomplish that which I purpose, and prosper in the thing for which I sent it."

Jesus' parables of the seed growing secretly (Mark 4:26–29), the wheat and the tares (Matthew 13:24–30), and the mustard seed (Mark 4:30–32) all suggest that the growth of the Kingdom of God, or progress in the life of faith, is somewhat hidden, like natural growth. Much of our deepest activity, our response to the challenge to develop a trusting acceptance of God, goes on wordlessly, almost unconsciously, at the depths of our awareness. It is God's doing more than our own, but the nature parables encourage us to trust that it is happening: "In short, the common world is pictured as a place of God's transforming presence."[19] Neither the New Testament nor most New Testament scholars draw ecological conclusions from the nature parables, but that doesn't mean such conclusions are not latent, waiting to be drawn by a new Christian theology of nature.

The Johannine Writings

The third major portion of the New Testament is the Johannine writings. An important motif in the gospel of John is that Jesus replaces the spaces that for Jews were sacred. Jesus is the new temple, the new locus of salvation. Thus the implication of the story of the healing at the pool of Siloam (John 9) seems to be that the old holy site of healing by water has been replaced by Jesus, the source of the new healing waters of baptism. In summarizing his study of such replacement texts W.D. Davies concludes: "Our discussion of the Fourth Gospel drives us back to the beginning of the Gospel to 1:14, where the flesh of Jesus of Nazareth is said to be the seat of the Logos: that Logos, whether as Wisdom or as Torah, is no longer attached to a land, as was the Torah, but to a Person who came to his own land, and was not received."[20] Like Paul and the Synoptics, John reworks the theme of the promised land.

However, both the Gospel of John and the epistles make a sharp contrast between the zone of the Spirit that Jesus' flesh centers and the zone of the world closed to the Spirit. Both are peculiarly "dualistic." The world is said not to know Christ or God (1:10, 17:25); Jesus is said not to be of this world (8:23); therefore Jesus' Kingdom cannot be of this world (18:36), and Jesus' disciples cannot belong to this world (15:19, 17:14). Still, God loved the world and sent the Son into the world (3:16–17, 12:47, 1 Jn 4:9). God did this to take away the world's sin (1:29, 1 Jn 2:2) and make Jesus the savior of the world (4:42, 1 Jn 4:14), the Light by which the world might find its true way (8:12). In no way therefore does this Johannine "dualism" imply that matter is evil. The contrast is between the tendency of space–time to resist God and the power of the Spirit to make space–time holy.

The Johannine stress on sacramentalism buttresses this interpretation. The Word becomes flesh so that the signs of God may become more pointed, more personal, more efficacious. Chapters 1–12 of the gospel depict Jesus working signs that testify to the divine power of love that fills his flesh. In transforming the water into wine, multiplying the loaves, discoursing on living water, and healing the man born blind, Jesus fills material things with the power of God. The Johannine community responsible for the gospel and the epistles probably rooted its high view of the Logos' enfleshment in a rich sacramental life. Every likelihood is that the Johannine allusions to baptism and the eucharist stem from a church that remembered Jesus' story in rich rituals. The sacraments were ways that Jesus could continue to heal and reveal, ways that God could continue to manifest his glory through material things. If ever one wanted a theology of manifestation, rich with the instinct that divinity expresses itself through all creation, the Johannine corpus provides it.

This is true also of the Apocalypse, that strange book written to intensify Christian faith in the midst of persecution. The Apocalypse is filled with natural symbols, many of them from the Old Testament, that its poetic author applies to a current situation of suffering. Interestingly, in several places the woes that the author predicts will come upon the wicked are deflected from nature: "Then I saw another angel ascend from the rising of the sun, with the seal of the living God, and he called with a loud voice to the four angels who had been given power to harm earth and sea, saying, 'Do not harm the earth or the sea or the trees, till we have sealed the servants of our God upon their foreheads.' " (7:2–3) Similarly, in chapter nine smoke comes from the locusts on earth and they are given the power of scorpions, but "they were told not to harm the grass of the earth or any green growth or any tree, but only those of mankind who have not the seal of God upon their foreheads." (9:4) When the vision of victory finally comes and the New Jerusalem is revealed, natural symbols again stand out: "Then he showed me the river of the water of life, bright as crystal, flowing from the throne of God and of the Lamb through the middle of the street of the city; also, on either side of the river, the tree of life with its twelve kinds of fruit, yielding its fruit each month; and the leaves of the tree were for the healing of the nations. Then shall no more be anything accursed. . . ." (22:1–3)

When shall no more anything be accursed? That might be the main ecological question the bible leaves us. How long, O Lord, how long before we grasp the contemporary implications of your presence in nature? The scriptural doctrines of creation and sacramentalism encourage the believer to gather nature under the fold of God's care, but the scriptural stresses on human salvation from sin and human beings' special place in God's plan have inclined many believers to neglect nature's rights and hopes. Thus one finds few references to ecological issues in representative recent surveys of New Testament ethics[21] or faith.[22] One therefore can accept James Barr's defense of the Old Testament against charges of being responsible for the ecological crisis[23] while continuing to wish that the positive biblical doctrines of nature had been better appropriated, developed, and applied.

Chapter Seven:
TRADITIONAL THEOLOGICAL DOCTRINES

The Apologists and Early Fathers

The earliest Christian theologians called upon to rework the evangelical notions of grace, sacramentalism, and a world capable of manifesting God were the apologists. In their theologies we see the beginnings of a two thousand year enterprise. As we are trying to do for our time, the apologists were trying to translate the key experiences and notions of Christian faith for their time, that faith might become vital and consoling. One of their prime topics was the doctrine of creation, and their approach to it directly bears on our theme.

Clement of Alexandria, for example, contrasted the views of Greek philosophers such as Plato with the bible's views of creation. Although on many points Clement was quite glad to confess a debt to the philosophers, he found the bible's understanding of creation far superior. The philosophers tended to deify the universe, rather than the creator of the universe. The biblical depiction of the world as coming solely from the volition of God was the more profound truth. God alone made the world, because God alone is divine in his being, capable of such an act. Where Platonic cosmology, following Plato's *Timaeus,* spoke of a Demiurge fashioning the world into its present shape, Clement said that God was his own Demiurge, both the source and the shaper of the world we now see.

It was Tertullian, however, who explicitly taught the doctrine of creation from nothingness. Tertullian conceded that this doctrine was not explicit in the bible, but he found it clearly implied. To place matter alongside God, to make matter co-eternal and co-existent with God, would encroach on God's sovereignty and freedom. True, creation from nothingness sharpens the point on the problem of evil, since it makes us ask whether God is the cause of the evil things that exist, but the alternatives to creation from nothingness are either a pantheism that would identify God and matter or a dualism of divinity and matter that would limit God's power.

Irenaeus was another early father who found biblical teaching to entail the notion of a single creator of all things. This view, which Irenaeus and others called God's "monarchy," fit well with the Old Testament depiction of God, and it provided a sharp contrast to the Greek notions of polytheism and pantheism. As well, it led the early fathers to criticize the Greek and Roman theories of history, which tended to be cyclic. Origen, for example, argued that if the Greek and Roman notions held good Moses would always be coming out of Egypt and Jesus would return endlessly to die on the cross. This jars with the biblical assumption that the events of Moses and Jesus were unique and decisive. Just as God creates each being, so God presides over a history in which each being's actions are significant, not merely a predictable part of a fated repetition.[1]

In his famous study of the social teachings of the Christian churches, Ernst Troeltsch emphasized the early importance of Stoic theories of natural law. Especially after Christians had won a measure of freedom from Roman persecution, theologians looked to Stoic teaching as a way to synthesize the fuller ethics they knew their entry into imperial life would call for. "As soon as the worst struggles were over and Christianity had to adjust its organization to the legal social system in general, the need was felt for a general theory of the basis and validity of the 'laws' which the Christians could accept. In this connection it was the apologists who, in addition to fusing the ethics of Christianity and of Stoicism, were also the first, at least to some extent, to bring the laws of the City of God into harmony with the laws of the city of this world. The Stoic idea of Natural Law, which the apologists regarded as identical with the Christian moral law, provided the way out of the difficulty."[2]

In the first two centuries or so after the apostles, then, Christian theologians sharpened the notions of creation and natural law. By stressing that God created the world from nothingness, they made God present to each creature, and made all creatures signs of God's power. In adapting the Stoic notion of Natural Law, they attributed the rationality by which nature moves, its regularity and harmony, to the divine mind. Indeed, often they took this natural regularity as a model for human affairs, arguing that human beings would do well to try to descry the divine reason guiding their peculiar natures, for if they would obey it all sorts of prosperity would follow. Of course it proved difficult to ascertain just what inbuilt laws God had imparted to human creatures, but the main conception held. If God was reasonable and human beings were God's creatures, then human beings must have been made with a plan, a purpose, a coding.

Despite their work on creation and natural law, however, the early apologists and fathers stood so close to the biblical and Greek discoveries of human beings' special privileges (covenant with God, reflective reason) that they could not make creation and natural law produce something parallel to archaic human beings' sense of being immersed in a sacred cosmos. A certain distancing, if not alienation, seems the price human beings had to pay for their special privileges.

The Later Fathers

Among the later fathers Augustine was the towering figure, his teachings on nature and grace virtually shaping Western Christian theology. In Augustine's view, God's freedom is paramount. Whether he creates, judges, redeems, or loves, God acts without any external necessity. That is because God is God: omnipotent, unlimited. As Jaroslav Pelikan has described Augustine's view, "The wisdom and power of God were such that even the evil deeds of evil men in defiance of his will eventually contributed to the achievement of his good and just purposes. The very name Omnipotent meant simply that God had the power to do everything he willed. It was above all in the mystery of creation that divine sovereignty made itself evident. Heaven and earth were subject to change and decay because they had been made out of nothing. 'We exist,' they would have to say, 'only because we have been made; we did not exist before we came to be so that we could have made ourselves.' Among the creatures, man was preeminently the object of the Creator's gracious intent. His creation was an act of sheer grace."[3]

The early Augustine drew much of his conception of God's creativity from Neoplatonic philosophy, but the mature Augustine was thoroughly molded by the bible, especially Genesis. Thus the mature Augustine clearly affirmed the gulf between the one Maker and the many things made. Still, he remained sufficiently influenced by Greek thought to speak of the divine essence as absolute and impassible. That God should change or suffer was unthinkable. Also unthinkable was the notion that anything should occur without God's power and choice. This led Augustine to a thoroughgoing doctrine of predestination. God was prescient, aware of things before they happen, arranging the future according to a knowledge which cannot be deceived or changed. The difference between this view and pagan fatalism is Augustine's inclusion of human causes in God's prescient scheme of how the future will unfold.

The upshot of predestination, and Augustine's theology as a whole, was a wholehearted praise of God's grace. God has made the world and guided it to its present state in utter freedom. The world is a magnificent testimony to God's goodness and power. So, despite an almost pessimistic view of human nature, which he considered to be deeply ravaged by sin, Augustine found creation marvelous. However, largely due to the limitations of the science of his time, he made little of the ecology of creation. And although he was curious about the natural world, Augustine did not praise it as a revelation equal to human history. Still, his sacramentalism made him prominent among the Catholic fathers who accepted the Johannine view that material things can become signs instituted by God to convey grace.[4]

In the East, the fathers associated with Nicene orthodoxy probably played the most influential role. Themselves disciples of Origen, the greatest of the Eastern speculative theologians, Athanasius and the Cappadocians (Basil, Gregory of Nyssa, and Gregory Nazianzus) checked the subordinationist dangers to which Origenist Christology was liable and firmly defended the divinity of the Logos and the spirit. "Nicaea took the Logos out of any conceivable intermediate position by bringing the belief that he is of the same essence as the ingenerate Father into the Creed and giving it central theological importance: what the Father is, that the Son is, and no less. The Logos is set firmly on the side of absolute deity. Arius, on the other hand, also setting out to affirm the total dichotomy between the ultimate source of things and everything which is derived from it, did so in the opposite way by assigning the Logos to the creatures' side of the gulf which separates them from absolute deity."[5]

Both the proponents of the position victorious at the Council of Nicaea (325) and their Arian opponents therefore were sensitive to the rights of divinity. Although they disagreed about the status of the Son, they agreed that a great gap yawned between the creator and his creatures. Probably Eastern notions of sacral rule played a strong part in this concern for the creator's rights. In a culture where the emperor was a great figure, holding the power of life and death over his subjects, people regarded their ruler with something close to awe. How much more awesome, then, must have seemed the power of the Emperor *par excellence,* the Pantocrator who ruled everything that existed. If the earthly ruler was carefully reverenced (indeed, worshiped in Roman religion), then the heavenly ruler deserved a cult of absolute purity, unsullied by any association of him with lowly creatures.

The orthodox retained a firm enough hold on the Incarnation and the sacraments to keep the world the site of God's manifestation, but in their divine liturgy one can see the seeds of a conception of the world in which temporal and natural affairs pale in comparison to heavenly matters. Among the peasants of the Eastern empire nature no doubt continued to be marvelous and close, but the Eastern theologians and church leaders began to develop a hieratic style that weakened a vigorous appreciation of nature.

The Medievals

Thomas Aquinas dominates the medieval West, through both the depth of his thought and the breadth of his later influence. A generation ago Etienne Gilson did heroic work in bringing the principles of what he called Aquinas' "Christian philosophy" before the contemporary West, and foremost among these principles was the primacy of the act of being. Aquinas above all was concerned with realities and, in the case of human beings, with the realities that people freely choose: "The only finite reality which the understanding can fruitfully explore is concrete being itself, the original, unique, and, in the case of man, unpredictable and free actualization of an inexhaustible essence by its own act-of-being. It is rather difficult to find in St. Thomas a single concrete problem whose solution is not ultimately based on this principle. He is primarily a theologian; and it is in constructing his theology with such striking technical originality that he best proves his fertility of mind. Wherever his philosophy touches his theology there is to be seen that new light with which the act-of-being illumines all it touches."[6]

For the understanding of creation, Thomas' focus on the act of being starkly underscores God's presence to the creature. God is the font of existence apart from whose influx the creature would not be. The chain of finite causes that shape *how* the creature exists cannot explain *that* the creature exists. Only the infinite cause, the source or font of existence, provides a sufficient reason for the existence of a creature, a being composed of act and lack (potency). Thomas seldom extends this principle ecologically, making God's creative influx of being the most prominent reality factor in the *network* of inanimate and animate beings. However, it would seem that we could move it in that direction, making God's preservation of creation the ultimate reality-factor in the processive or evolutionary network that links all the members of an ecosphere.

Aquinas' notion of analogy dovetails with his stress on the act of being, and it provides him a balanced view of the creator–creature relation. For Thomas analogy is only a faint tie to the mysterious God, not at all something that allows reason to pry into the divine nature. But it is enough to make our inference that God exists quite reasonable. The creative source must be somewhat like its created effect, and this likeness ultimately pivots on the act of being. By sharing in the reality, the existence, the being that God alone possesses independently, we creatures manifest a likeness to God. We are unlike God in being distinct, limited possessors of being. The essence that gives us our distinct identity has no strict parallel in God, whose "essence" is to exist unlimitedly. But the real foundation of our beings in God, and the clarification it brings us to think of God as a something or someone whose "essence" or whatness or central characteristic is unlimited existence, provide a connection between what we are and what God is. I find this connection one of the most promising leads the tradition offers a contemporary theology of nature, for were we properly to exploit it, we might make ecology alive with the immanence of God.

During the medieval period the East also was discussing the philosophy of creation, trying to assimilate its Hellenistic heritage to Christian faith. In the twelfth century Michael Psellus was probably the outstanding representative of Christian Hellenism. Psellus revered the achievements of Plato, but his first allegiance was to Christian faith. So he set about correcting the Greek philosophers' notions of God and creation, in the light of evangelical notions. This meant qualifying the sense in which we can speak of the world as one, and making it clear that God's being is unique. As Pelikan describes Psellus' position: "The oneness of God was transcendent, beyond all number and beyond simplicity itself, so that ultimately the cosmos could be called 'one' only on account of its participation as creature in the oneness of the Creator. Similarly, God was the beginning (*arche*) of all beings, not in the sense that he was the first in a series, but in the sense that he transcended all being and that all beings were dependent on him. It was orthodox doctrine that God was 'beyond and above all things that are known and all things that exist.' The distinction as well as the link between the Creator and his creation had to be maintained: immanence without pantheistic identification, transcendence without deistic isolation."[7]

West and East, then, one finds the medieval theologians using the Greek philosophy made available to them by the Arabs to refine their doctrine of creation. Analyzing the makeup of creatures, they came to stress the being that creatures could only derive from God and God's unique existential status as far beyond creatures yet creatures' inmost ground. Thus the brilliant reflections of the medievals did not lead to the removal of God's mystery. The more they applied philosophical tools to the analysis of the creator–creature relationship, the more the medievals came away magnifying the power of the creator. The creator was of another order, at a rank human investigators could never understand. The creator was intrinsically mysterious, by his inmost being too rich for the human investigator to fathom. The mystical theology of Dionysius the Areopagite that greatly influenced Aquinas influenced the Eastern Church even more, because Dionysius made the divine mystery an overshadowing of the mind that beckoned the theologian to mystical prayer.[8]

The Reformers

The Protestant Reformation of the sixteenth century challenged the medieval notion that nature and grace, reason and faith, could stand in a harmonious balance. The Protestant hunger for a more effective religious sense of salvation tended to brush the capacities of reason aside, pushing forward the greater riches of faith. This appears, for example, in Luther's reflections on the hiddenness of God and God's revelation. Only from the cross does God show us the depths of the

divine nature, and even there the showing is veiled, the revelation hidden. For Luther the knowledge of God that we can
derive from nature pales compared to the knowledge we can
derive from faith in Christ. Thus it would not be hard to deni-
grate the inferential or analogical knowledge nature furnishes, or to ignore the significance of the act of being that
makes God present in the inmost reality of all creatures.

For example, Benjamin Drewery has described Luther's
views on the knowledge of God as follows: "Fundamentally, if
the God we seek to know is the One God and Father of our
Lord Jesus Christ, then all knowledge of Him—'general' or
'proper'—must be of His own self-giving, prior to, undercut-
ting, re-aligning, over-arching all our human seeking. Hence
this 'general' knowledge—whatever its content—cannot be opposed to, or complementary to, or a 'concession' allowed by,
this 'proper' knowledge. God is One and His knowledge is
wholly of His grace. Such knowledge is never merely academic
or curious, but salvation itself; and salvation is wholly of
Christ and through faith. Any knowledge springing from any
other source is knowledge of a false god—an idol of our making, whether a concrete figure of anthropomorphic worship or
an abstract intellectual formulation."[9]

Despite this check on natural theology, Lutheran theology often found strong emotional resonances in nature, and its
biblical orientation provided it the naturalistic reflection of
both testaments, from the Psalms to Colossians. Nonetheless,
Lutheranism generally suggested a split or antagonism between the mind with which one studies the world and the
mind with which one pursues (or responds to) God.

Calvin retained a great emphasis on the need for biblical
revelation, but he also valued the knowledge of God's creatorship that nature (as well as scripture) provides. Thus John
McNeill has described a two-fold Calvinist revelation: "God
makes Himself known to man in a two-fold revelation. He is
known as Creator, both through the outward universe and
through Holy Scripture: He is known as Redeemer through
the Scripture alone. This distinction had such growing importance for Calvin that, according to E. A. Dowey, Jr., it con-

trolled the structure of the *Institutes* in the final Latin edition. Man is himself a part of that created world through which God is made known. The ordered array of the heavenly host, the symmetry and beauty of the human body, the versatility and inventiveness of the mind are testimonies of God, and His acts of justice and mercy in experience and history invite us to acquire a knowledge of Him. Yet through the perversity of our natures we 'turn upside down' these intimations of God and set up as the object of our worship 'the dream and phantom of our own brain.' Not on the basis of the light of nature but through the revelation of the Word we gain a true and saving knowledge of God. [Yet] Calvin's world, from stars to insects, from archangels to infants, is the realm of God's sovereignty. A reverent awe of God breathes through all his work."[10]

The Protestant challenge to the embellishments of faith and worship that had grown up by the sixteenth century drew a spirited response from both Roman and Eastern Orthodox theologians. The Council of Trent reaffirmed and clarified what it took to be the Catholic tradition regarding the sacraments, while the Eastern Orthodox defended both the sacraments and their tradition of iconography. This led to some interesting refinements, for example of the relation between icons and the eucharist: ". . . while the worship paid to the icons was one of honor rather than of adoration, the worship paid to the Eucharist was one of adoration rather than merely of honor, because the presence in the Eucharist was that of the Lord himself. Similarly, when it came to the definition of the presence, it would not suffice to say that the body and blood of Christ were present 'in a manner appropriate to symbols or icons' . . . for the presence was more real than such terms could express. Just how real the presence was, Eastern theology had to learn from the West to describe with precision; this was apparently how it acquired the Greek word for 'transubstantiation (*metousiosis*),' which now became a technical term in Eastern theology."[11]

Protestant doctrinal theology therefore pressured all the churches for further clarification of a number of issues relevant to the theology of nature. The value of natural revelation, the reverent sense of God's presence in nature that biblical faith could inspire, and the status of material creatures as means of God's manifestations all clamored for reconsideration. The general effect of the leading Reformers' own efforts, however, was to rivet attention on the biblical, especially the Pauline, concern with justification and faith. In the brilliant light of this concern, natural theology somewhat fell to the sidelines.

The Moderns

The Renaissance, the Enlightenment, and the development of Newtonian science all contributed to a new interest in nature and a new conception of nature's significance. In modern philosophy, the leading figures considered themselves emancipated from the doctrines of faith and free to develop new views of nature. Thus Descartes established a dualism between the human mind and the natural world, Spinoza and Leibniz tried to overcome this dualism, Berkeley rejected the notion of material substances, Kant made the mind the source of the laws of nature, and Hegel subordinated material nature to the ends of the Absolute Spirit.[12]

Natural scientists themselves often spoke as though they could only be free to investigate nature if they threw off the shackles of Christian faith, but Stanley Jaki has argued in some detail that the assumptions of Christian faith were intrinsic to the enterprise of modern science. Specifically, modern science only arose in the orbit of Christian civilization, where it was a common assumption that the world was knowable, because it was a common assumption that the world was the creation of an intelligent, provident, and good God.[13]

The religious reactions to the rise of modern science varied, liberals tending to accept the advances and conservatives tending to reject them as godless. Insofar as Newtonian science seemed to depict the world as a closed mechanical system, it gave some plausibility to inferences such as Laplace's that God was no longer a necessary hypothesis. Newton himself retained God, though not the God of orthodox Christian faith, but by the time scientists had developed the biology and geology of the nineteenth century, the intellectual establishment was at best Deistic, consigning God to a vague role in the origins of a universe now quite self-sufficient.

American religious thought, as William Clebsch has interpreted it, played interesting variations on the modern reaction. In Jonathan Edwards, Ralph Waldo Emerson, and William James, one can see an aesthetico-religious outlook reverently appreciative of nature's beauties, which it considered reflections of the world's ultimate source.

Edwards was perhaps the most brilliant scion of the Calvinist movement, and probably America's most innovative theologian. Where the Puritans had generally stressed ethics, he tried to portray Christianity as the way to a beautiful life: "Perhaps we can appreciate the revolutionary nature of Edwards' achievement in translating Puritan religion from the language of ethics into the language of esthetics if we *re*translate his concept of living a beautiful life back into the idiom of moralistic Christianity. There the virtuous person enjoys God and uses the world; the corrupt person uses God and enjoys the world. Edwards recoiled from the notion that we might use God, just as he recoiled from the doctrine that we should not enjoy the world. The beauty of God and the beauty of all created beings impressed itself on him as a single, indivisible beauty. Truly virtuous men and women, sensing that they had been given a new frame of mind, both enjoyed God and enjoyed God's world."[14]

Emerson was perhaps the most naturalistic of the great American religious philosophers, his idealistic bent inclining him to find God immanent in nature, and his Unitarian bent inclining him away from orthodox Christian conceptions of God and Jesus. His book *Nature,* published anonymously in 1836, portrayed the physical world as welcoming human beings into a fulfilling contemplation. The stars, the woods, even a bare common, bleak at twilight under a clouded sky, offered human beings a delightful repose. At times nature would find us sorrowful, or even would contribute to our sorrows, but overall Emerson found the universe friendly.

William James tended to make God's existence dependent upon human beings' religious experiences, but a night of intense religious experience on Mount Marcy in New Hampshire in 1898 burned into his soul the power of the divinity that the "nature mythologies" had long proclaimed. As Clebsch reports it, "Just after the experience on Mount Marcy, he could not 'find a single word for all that significance, and don't know what it was significant of, so there remains a mere boulder of *impression*' ... [Later] James distinguished the 'two kinds of Gods' and related them to one another as the environing and the indwelling Gods, or, more profoundly, the God of mankind's cosmic consciousness and the (same) God coming into a particular person's consciousness. One's consciousness retained the significance of crucial religious experiences, and this sense of significance could be released from the storehouse of memory when sensations lowered the threshold of consciousness to allow an entry of 'the great cosmic consciousness in which we live.' "[15]

Thus spake America's great psychologist of religious experience, enouncing one of modernity's major theses: *we* interpret nature (and society, and the self) in ways that sometimes confer religious significance on them. The question of God's objective or independent action in nature, society, or the self is at best obscure, at worst fallaciously put. This thesis does not pass muster in today's post-modern situation, but its evolution was a major plot-line of the natural theology that developed between the Reformation and the mid-twentieth century.

Our Contemporaries

In this century such scientific developments as relativity physics and quantum mechanics, along with stunning advances in astronomy, genetics, and subatomic physics, have broken the mechanistic mold of nineteenth century science. Ecology, interrelation, has become a mind-set, helping more and more of our contemporaries to think holistically, in terms of interconnections. Charles Birch, an Australian biologist and process thinker, has developed eight theses that express the convictions of many contemporary naturalists. First, the world-view we take from science reflects the main assumptions of the society in which we live. Because our society has been bent on mastering the physical world, our socio-scientific view of reality has been that of conquerers wanting to subjugate something outside themselves, something almost considered an enemy. Second, our worldview has pictured nature as a contrivance, the result of a set of accidents. Thus nature has become a sort of mindless factory that human beings are called to control. Third, the Christian theology of the West, where most contemporary science has developed, has largely accommodated to this imperialist view, severing nature's connections with humanity and God. Fourth, many of our contemporaries finally have started to realize that this conquistadorial attitude is dysfunctional, ugly and unecological.

Fifth, when one encounters the world freshly and personally, it is not at all a warehouse but rather something mysterious and wonderful. Unfortunately, most of the people encountering science freshly and personally today are neither scientists nor Christians. Sixth, if science and faith are going to deal with the natural world adequately in the future, they will have to change their relation to one another, becoming allies rather than adversaries. Seventh, the beginnings of this alliance suggest a new view of creation that takes creation's unity seriously. Ecological, this new view keeps nature, humanity, and divinity in relation to one another. It does not opt for science *or* humanistic insights but insists that both approaches have irreplaceable contributions to make. Eighth, the ecological or interrelational view of creation now emerging should entail a sharpened sense of responsibility for all of life. If we heed this ethical implication and build upon it, we may be able to develop a global society both sustainable and just.[16]

The new ecological view of nature and ethics that Birch summarizes has antecedents in the prior Christian tradition, as I hope our doctrinal sketch suggests, but it takes a quantum leap beyond what the mainline of the tradition has offered. Today many environmentalists want to lessen the gap between human beings and the rest of nature, so that nature has more rights. Both theologically and in the human courts, our ecological co-existence with nature should move us to consider nature an intimate and essential partner, not just our servant or slave. We shall take systematic note of this point in the next chapter, but here the question might be how representative this doctrinal suggestion is. My impression is that ecological convictions now have a widespread general following, but that they have yet to penetrate the churches' doctrinal assumptions sufficiently to make the churches effective exponents of an ecological ethics or worldview.

For example, I note that neither "ecology" nor "nature" (in the sense of the physical world) occurs in *Dictionary of the Council,* the guide to Vatican II edited by J. Deretz and A. Nocent.[17] All nine of the references to "creation" have an anthropocentric cast, the most ecological of them (from the decree on revelation, #3) reading: "God, who through the Word creates all things (cf. Jn. 1:3) and keeps them in existence, gives men an enduring witness to Himself in created realities (cf. Rom. 1:19–20)." References to the physical sciences are slight, the most relevant being the statement from *Gaudium et Spes* (#33) that "through his labors and his native endowments man has ceaselessly striven to better his life. Today, however, especially with the help of science and technology, he has extended his mastery over nearly the whole of nature and continues to do so." The non-judgmental character of this statement suggests that the council fathers were not greatly preoccupied with the ecological havoc that human beings' ceaseless strivings lately have wreaked.

Pope John Paul II's commentary on the Vatican II documents does not have index-entries for "ecology" or "environment," but it does have a short chapter entitled "The Consciousness of Creation" in which we read: "The Council teaches explicitly that God 'provides men with constant evidence of himself in created realities' (DV 3). The term 'evidence' is particularly significant because it indicates the element of revelation in creation itself, which is, as it were, the first and fundamental expression of God, by which he speaks to us and calls for the response of faith."[18] There is a thin reference to the natural world in John Paul II's section on "the eschatological character of the Church and the renewal of the world," but no mention of science or technology in the index. The Pope's encyclicals have done a little better than his commentary, but none of the three encyclicals issued to date would win a blue ribbon for ecological farsightedness. Thus, it is not hard to make the argument that the Catholic Church needs a new theology of nature.

Chapter Eight:
A SYSTEMATIC APPROACH

From Doctrines to Systematics

In Part Two we are concerned with constructive theology, an effort to speak forth how Christian faith might best regard nature in view of today's insights and problems. After laying a foundation in Christian conversion, we spent two chapters on doctrines, summarizing some of the main points one finds in Christian scripture and traditional theology. Now our task shifts, becoming more speculative. Retaining the foundational horizon of conversion to Christ, we must try to set the high points of the doctrinal tradition into cogent correlation, so as to render "nature" as clear and significant a term as possible.

Before starting this systematic work, however, it seems necessary to prefix several cautions. First, our two chapters on the Christian doctrines of nature are far from exhaustive. Not only do they span the nearly three thousand years from the earliest portions of the Hebrew Bible to the present, perforce they only skim the surface of any given biblical subsection or historical period. An expert could write a huge tome on the conception of nature in the Psalms or the writings of Augustine, so obviously our brief surveys have limited weight. Nonetheless, they do provide a miniature version of what Christian faith has developed or contended with in its long efforts to situate itself in the world.

Second, much of what the tradition has said about nature has reflected suppositions that do not hold today, at least not with the vigor they had in the past. For example, there has been a major shift from the anthropocentrism of the bible and most of the tradition to today's holistic views. In the bible and most of the tradition, the world revolves around human beings. Even when the bible makes much more of God than it does of human beings, it makes much more of human beings than it does of nature. This is understandable, granted the bible's fascination with the covenant God struck with Israel and the redemption God worked through Christ. It made sense through most of the tradition, when the earth that human beings were filling and subduing seemed to be the center of the universe. But when the Copernican revolution came, and then such successor shocks as Darwinian evolution and Einsteinian relativity, human beings' prominence started to fade. Of course the heroics and foibles of our kind continued to fascinate all the members of the tribe, but objectively, in terms of how we began to construct the world, human preeminence started to fade in modern times. Today a strong current of opinion says that we are not the center of the world. We are not the oldest of the species and, as the significance of our wars and despoiliations of nature starts to impress itself upon the general populace, it is debatable that we are the most admirable of the species. Anthropocentrism therefore can seem a gigantic self-indulgence. Perhaps it made sense when *homo sapiens* was in its adolescence, but if we are to come of age it will have to go.

That is the way many of our contemporaries might sketch the shift in our consciousness of nature, and it sets the systematician an important part of her agenda. To make sense to our generation, a translation of the traditional Christian doctrines of nature probably has to lean heavily on the places where God predominates over human beings and non-human creation receives an appreciative hearing. The places where human beings have a commission to subdue the earth, or where the earth lies at humanity's beck and call, will not win many kudos from environmentalists. This does not mean, of course, that the systematician can neglect the importance that either the tradition or contemporary ecological analyses place on human agency. The tradition's notion that human beings are special images of God, and the contemporary ecological intuition that human beings are the lethal factor capable of ruining the whole earth, both put pressure on the systematician to give human agency close attention.[1]

A third caution concerns the nature of systematic work itself. Where doctrinal studies can be rather factual, because sufficient historical work usually can determine what a given author or period thought about a given topic, systematic studies are hypothetical. The systematician does not lay down definitively how reality is shaped or what Christian faith entails. Rather he or she tries through creative imagination to isolate the major ingredients in a given theological problem, establish their internal correlations, and develop a coherent vision or sketch or construction that stimulates insight, understanding, in which the problem clarifies or is solved.[2] As new data come in, or further reflection shows more ramifications in one of the key relationships, or fresh imagination throws up alternate images and schemes, the systematician's hypothetical solution to a problem may come to need considerable revision. It is parallel to the natural scientist's work: an explanation of a given phenomenon is only as good as its clarification of the relevant data. With this caveat in mind, let us now attack some of the key problems blocking our way to a satisfactory contemporary theology of nature.

The Ontological Core

At the center of any theology of creation I would find adequate is God's endowment of being. All that exists, inanimate and animate, non-human and human, depends directly on God, only exists or is real because of the divine largess. Because they were sensitive to this dependency, archaic people found everything fraught with significance. The Holy, the Really-Real, the Ultimate that made the world solid could manifest itself in the storm or the calm, the rock or the sea, the king or the beggar. Let any reality catch an unusual angle of light, tip slightly from its accustomed slot, and it would become revelatory. The mystery of being, the ultimate force both awesome and fascinating, was as near as the stirring of the wind, as shaking as a vivid dream.

Archaic people tended to stress the gripping details of such revelations, but beneath their imaginative reports one senses a firm instinct for the heart of the matter. The heart of the matter is the mystery of ex-sistence, the primordial fact that we stand forth from nothingness. Why is there something rather than nothing? Why does this man (or house, or turtle) exist, when its limitation and vulnerability show that it could very easily not exist, that its reality should not at all be taken for granted?

The Christian bible and tradition accepted much of this archaic mentality, not at all wanting faith in a transcendent God independent of the world to weaken human beings' awe before the mystery of being. The things of the world come from the world's source, so they are vestiges or images of the source. From the things God has made we can infer something of the divine nature, a bit of its wisdom and power.

For the deeper fathers and medievals, every creature directly depended on the creator, drawing its being from the sole font of being, the sole reality that is uncaused. That meant that every creature was a presence of God. As Augustine put it, God is more intimate to me than I am to myself. When I return to myself, try to swim down to the depths of my being, I find that God has preceded me. Were there no God to found my reality, I would float in mere possibility. The fact that I actually exist, that I am real rather than merely possible, testifies to God's ongoing grant of being.

In modern times philosophy grew leery of the doctrine of existence, and science shouted that we should pay attention to secondary causes, the forces that shape how beings change, how evolution does its business. Bracketing the questions that radiate from existence, the moderns did splendid work on essence, showing the world to be much richer, much more complicated, dynamic, and ancient, than the medievals had ever suspected.

Today the existential questions have returned. Finding that their studies of how things change have not brought sufficient wisdom to make the world meaningful, many contemporary thinkers have taken up a post-modern interest in being.

Indeed, one can even read the current obsession with hermeneutics (interpretation) as a new form of the old interest in revelation or manifestation. Where archaic and biblical peoples looked to the skies, the tribal ceremonies, or the striking experiences of extraordinary individuals for manifestations of the divine, our contemporaries pore over texts and monuments, fascinated by the diverse ways things acquire significance, the inexhaustible capacity of the human spirit to transmit meaning and receive it.

Building on Christian conversion and doctrine, I would have a new theology of nature lay great stress on existence. The being of natural things, their standing-forth from nothingness in such a variety of forms, is a bedrock wonder theology should constantly ponder. All creation is gratuitous. Neither we nor the Everglades had to be. To make either us or the Everglades took a direct and comprehensive act of God, and that act of God is the most important thing about us. Moment by moment, God ratifies his creative intent to have this evolving world. At every frame in their motion picture, the Everglades shout that wonderful, mysterious powers are at hand. Aristotle said that philosophy, the life in love with wisdom, begins with wonder. We can say the same for an adequate theology of nature. The first word on the good natural theologian's lips is the *mysteriousness* of reality. The first stirrings in his heart are toward awe, gratitude, and reverence. Nature is not brute stuff, the haphazard spill of a cosmic dumpster. Nature shows God's serious play, God's love of profusion, God's desire to hurl the divine Is! to the outermost galaxies.

So the theology of nature beckoning us today is resolutely contemplative. Before it begins to analyze the relations of nature to God, society, the self, or Christ, the new theology I want will pause for some wordless appreciation. For until it sees an El Capitan, hears the ocean crashing at a Gloucester, feels the wind rippling through the prairies, smells a cluster of spring flowers, or tastes fresh berries, a theology of nature doesn't know its subject matter. Useful and destructive, consoling and threatening, nature above all ex-sists, is, dances before us, issues a cornucopia of wonders. At the head of our new books it should be written that God is with us in very diverse ways, pouring himself forth in prodigal nature.

Christological Motifs

The ontological core is most luminous when faith frees us from the blinders of purely technical reason. Casting off the will to power, contemplative faith insists that nature first deserves appreciation, participation, and recognition as a system of fellow beings. If this first moment does not provide technology its context, technology will make nature a wasteland.

The presence of Christ in the physical world is only luminous by the power of faith. To ascribe the intelligibility of nature to the Logos of the Triune God takes us far beyond the evidences admissible in a science textbook. Yet Christians have long pondered the eternal reason finally responsible for the intelligible processes of the physical world, and they have long realized that the Incarnation forces them to relate this eternal reason to Jesus, the Word become flesh. So in this section we think of what might color the ontological core gold with the Incarnation, red with the Passion, green with the Resurrection.

The being that creation receives from God is divine. According to much of the tradition, what separates creation from God is non-being. Finitude, mortality, ignorance, and evil are all species of non-being. I am not going to argue this point. The reader should be aware that many modern and contemporary analysts have disputed it, for reasons both good and bad. I am simply going to keep building my own systematic theology of nature, which stresses creation's divinity and correlates this divinity with the logical character of the Christian God.

If creatures derive from the Christian God, they come stamped with the modalities of the Father, the Son, and the Spirit. However those modalities should be reformulated for a feminist time, the fathomless, reasonable, and inspirational overtones they bear seem wholly retainable. Nature, as well as humanity, reflects its trinitarian source. The divinity designated by the scriptural "Father" is like the Greek *apeiron,* unbounded and (in our terms) unformed. The divinity designated by the traditional "Son" is expressive, lightsome, and "increasing." The divinity designated by the traditional "Spirit" is loving, encircling, nurturing, defending, and atoning.

Christians have not tended to look at nature with these trinitarian lens, but that doesn't mean they could not or should not. In our time, nature has become more mysterious, uncanny, and surprising than it was even two generations ago. In current astronomical speculation, for instance, some prominent hypotheses (black holes, parallel universes) are too weird initially to accredit. Thus nature is clamoring to be seen through new lenses. Sometimes it seems to shift like a kaleidoscope. Here, however, I want to concentrate on the Christological colorations of nature's ontological core, because those have the strongest sanction from the biblical tradition. For example, in the Pauline and Johannine theologies, creation holds together in the filial Word. All things were made through him; he is the alpha and omega of the creativity that lets all things be.

If God expresses the divine reality fully, in an eternal self-manifestation, and if creation is a partial expression of God, temporal and processive, then we can picture the creative process as a temporal subset or inset or derivative stream of the full, eternal self-expression. Creation occurs in the Son, the Word, because the Son, the Word, is God's utter self-expression. When the Johannine Jesus says "I am," evoking Yahweh's "I am who am," he gives human voice to a divine self-expression so utter that probably it is silent. All expressions of the divine fontal source collocate within this primordial expression of *the* Word. Thus, all expressions are logical, derivative, and reflective of their source on the model or in the contrails of *the* Word.

Creation therefore comes from God somewhat the way that God utters an eternal act of self-knowing, and it returns to God somewhat the way that the Word fuses with the Father in the Spirit. We can distinguish Father, Son, and Spirit relationally, and we can really distinguish creation from its trinitarian creator, but in both cases the community, the shared being, should be equally to the fore. God is One, as well as Three. God is one with creation, as well as apart from creation. Nowadays the transcendent God may seldom speak dramatically, but the God immanent in nature is never silent, never not addressing our senses, our minds, our hearts. Insofar as God is one with natural creation, nature is God's constant manifestation, expression, and performance. Nietzsche demanded that God dance and sing. God sang and danced every day at Tinker Creek, when Annie Dillard was there to give audience. Whenever we wish, we can catch overtones of the cosmic Christ, the creative reason that Jesus touchingly humanized. The Word is always broadcasting.

So our contemporaries' recent depressions about the silence of God, the absence of God, tell in large part of their loss of natural sensitivity. When we follow our instinct that every light in our minds, every color before our eyes, comes from the mystery of being, we find the world brimming with divinity, too rich for our puny ciphers. Then the gold and red and green of the incarnate Word become more valuable, since we feel great need for a master text, a set of primary colors. And this then sets the Incarnation back where the bible and early fathers had it, in the midst of natural creation. There history and ecology are not antinomies. There both are beacons to God.

History and Ecology in God

Stressing ontology and Christology, we have come to a theology that places nature in the trinitarian God. In this section I hope to solidify this position, by reflecting further on the primacy of the divine being.

For the past several generations, during which biblical studies have flourished, it has been fashionable to speak of God's lordship of history. Retrieving the scriptural faith that God acts, makes a difference, is not inert, biblical scholars and theologians have tried to understand what the divine action, difference, or liveliness might be like, especially during a season when many thought God dead, silent, or missing. The impact of this recent work in biblical theology has been significant, shaping, for example, liberation theology's convictions that God fights against evil, fights for the world's oppressed. Still, the willingness of some biblical theologians to build walls between "Greek" philosophy and "Israelite" faith, or between nature and history, has shriveled the significance of God's action and set up spurious human conflicts.

If there is One God, as Israel's *shema* (Deuteronomy 6) proclaims, then divinity's relations to history and nature must be similar, and likely they are not limited to the categories developed by the bible. Further, if the One God cares for, lures forward, all her children, then philosophy and faith are neither limited to the Greek and Israelite modes nor set against one another as implacable foes. Eric Voegelin has done the masterwork detonating such false dichotomies, showing that what he calls the noetic and pneumatic differentiations of consciousness are both potentially universal and intrinsically complementary.[3]

As a further consequence of his meditations on these central matters, Voegelin has also concluded that reality forms a universal Whole, which "happens" in God: "The various strata of reality with their specific time-dimensions, furthermore, are not autonomous entities but form, through the relations of foundation and organization, the hierarchy of being which extends from the inorganic stratum, through the vegetative and animal realms, to the existence of man in his tension toward the divine ground of being. There is a process of the Whole of which the In-Between reality with its process of history is no more than a part, though the very important part in which the process of the Whole becomes luminous for the eschatological movement beyond its own structure. Within this process of the Whole, then, some things, as for instance the earth, outlast other things, as for instance the individual human beings who inhabit the earth; and what we call 'time' without further qualifications is the mode of lastingness peculiar to the astrophysical universe which permits its dimension of time to be measured by its movements in space. But even this ultimate mode of lastingness to which as a measure we refer the lastingness of all other things, is not a 'time' in which things happen, but the time-dimension of a thing within the Whole that also comprises the divine reality whose mode of lastingness we express by such symbols as 'eternity.' Things do not happen in the astrophysical universe; the universe, together with all things founded in it, happens in God."[4]

The passage demands exegesis, for it is near the culmination of more than three hundred pages of dense intellectual history. First, the various strata of reality are the traditional chain of being, from rocks to angels. Second, these different strata of beings, with all the creatures they contain, form a whole. Discrete as they may appear when viewed from below, a comprehensive view shows them so manifoldly related as to comprise a single mega-system. Third, the developments in this mega-system include the processes of the human realm, where consciousness discovers itself to be Plato's Metaxy (In-Between). Human light only is competent between the *apeiron* from which formed realities derive and the divine Goodness toward which formed realities move. Nonetheless, human light is enough to disclose that the whole universal process is in labor to reach a consummating conclusion that will take it beyond itself. For Christian faith, this "beyond" is a definitive attainment of God, a once-for-all repose in the divine love.

Fourth, we speak of "time" to describe the way that the beings of the astrophysical universe perdure, but we should not picture "time" as the matrix in which things happen. Rather, "eternity," the way that divinity perdures, is the matrix in which things happen. Time is only a partial medium or foundation. The full medium or foundation of the universe is the divine creativity that lets it be. Thus it is misleading or short-sighted to speak of God's actions in history, if such speech leads to imagining history or time as something into which God must irrupt. On the contrary, history reposes in God, as do all the beings of time, all the creatures composing the astrophysical universe. God is the greater and they are the lesser. God is the Whole, and they are the parts. There is not more being because God has created. There is no history or ecology that is not finally a species of theology. Nature is not God, but God is the inmost being of all nature's processes, connections, and individual entities. Creation holds together in the Word, draws breath from the Spirit, and skates on a time that is but a thin ice stretched over the parental infinity.

Nature and the Divine Impersonality

Process theology has labored heroically to bring Christian doctrine and current science into harmony, but the tendency of process theologians to limit God convinces me that the theology of nature I seek will not come in process categories.[5] Useful as those categories are for honoring the interrelatedness of all creatures, they seem not to grasp the ontological core. The basic mystery of creation is how there can be limitation, finite participation in being. One doesn't illumine this basic mystery by placing the surd portion in God, creation's ultimate reason.

On the other hand, the process theologians have tended to stand against the hard-shelled biblicists and speak up for God's impersonal presences in nature. To be sure, disjunctions between history and nature, personal and impersonal, finally break down in God's case, because of the divine simplicity. But the process theologians' greater interest in the physical world has made them more receptive to the divine impersonality than the biblicists have tended to be. Since I find fruitful ties between the divine impersonality and Asian religious thought, I want to connect my theology of nature with the "world theology" that scholars such as Wilfred Cantwell Smith have begun to sketch.[6]

The unity of God, leading to the omnipresence of what Karl Rahner has called transcendental revelation,[7] forces us to take Asian religious experience more seriously than classical Christian theology did. For example, Hindu, Buddhist, and Taoist philosophies all offer rich reflections on nature that Christian theologians have yet to appropriate. In East Asia, where Buddhist and Taoist cosmologies have held sway, ultimate reality has been rather impersonal. Nirvana and the Tao both have reflected more of nature's dispassion than human beings' sufferings and joys. In each case, the path of religious development has carried the generous disciple from a loss of ego to a union with nature. Nature coincided with ultimate reality. Nirvana, the ultimate, became the inmost reality of samsara, the relative and changing. The Tao that could be named was not the real Tao, the moving force so ultimate it was the condition for any naming.

Because their societies set human affairs against the backdrop of a much more impressive natural world, Asian Buddhists and Taoists tried to make physical creation a congenial home. They had no commission to subdue this creation, no sacred writ suggesting their human account was vastly more important. At times they abused nature, deforesting or eroding the land. But on the whole East Asians' aesthetico-religious desire for harmony with nature made them respectful, inclined to look to nature for the way to peace.

The classical Taoists were striking poets, and their images resonate yet. Lao Tzu found nature reversing many human spontaneities, so he praised the uncarved block, the valley, the female, the infant, and the empty, because nature seemed to honor them with survival or ultimate power. Chuang Tzu stressed unity with the Great Clod, the Whole of nature's processes. For him death was natural and most human culture was contrived. The way to peace led through obscurity and inner "fasting." Fame and outer busyness usually led to grief. As for Lao Tzu, not-doing was more important than doing. Not-doing meant dancing to nature's lead, flowing with nature's grain.

Any Christian whose theology of grace is up-to-date will suspect that these classical East Asian views have been potent revelations. Through them millions of human beings have found consolation and peace. Indeed, they are often reminiscent of Western contemplative views, especially in their stress on unknowing and diminishing the ego. When we empty the spirit of the pretense and greed infecting most societies' educations, the spirit not only senses the richness of no-thing-ness and simplicity, it also becomes poetic, finding inner emptiness a womb of vivid imagery. Thus Francis' poverty led to songs to Brother Sun and Sister Moon, John of the Cross' *nada* led to spiritual canticles, and many an anchorite fled into nature's silent beauty to pray psalms to God.[8] From the bible the Western contemplatives retained a preference for personal categories, but they knew from experience that God comes in dark nights, clouds of unknowing, that call personal categories into serious question. Thus they grew poised to find God in all things, to find a single divine love streaming down from the Father of all lights.

Nature testifies to God's impersonality. There are ways of being, production, intelligibility, and life that do not center in a reflective self. These ways are far from the whole story about God. For Christians they will always be less eloquent than Jesus. But they are essential chapters in the story, especially for a time on the brink of ecological disaster. Today stressing the impersonality of God in nature might lower our lethal weapons a fraction. Today it might reassert the priority of being-with, lessen the force of doing-against. Then, rightly ordered to a nature again considered sacral, we might treat creation more as God probably intended when he made the morning stars sing together and all the angels shout for joy.

Sacramentalism and the Cosmological Myth

I have been elaborating the innermost concepts of the new Christian theology of nature I sense aborning. My candidates have been the primal act of being, the eternal generation of the Logos, God's envelopment of history and ecology, and the divine impersonality that nature presents. These inner concepts link in sacramentality. My systematics of nature translates the Christian tradition for our time, and gears up for an ecological ethics, by stressing nature's powers of manifestation. When we begin to see nature afresh, honoring its expressions of the divine mystery, we shall start on the road to the theory and practice our times demand.

I do not mean, of course, that emphases other than the sacramental have no place. One of today's happy features is the plurality of insights the theologian can honor, and the freedom this pluralism holds out. Knowing that fellow workers from other traditions likely will see the problems in my perspective, and likely will offer complements or correctives, I am free to develop my own deepest instincts, which run toward sacramentality.

As we have seen, sacramentality is not a new notion. Most traditional religions have espoused it, traditional Christianity very prominently included. But today sacramentality offers the West special therapies. Since the Enlightenment, when reason broke through to new autonomies and the empirical emphases of physical science earned special praise, the West has been struggling with a manifold dividedness. A Heidegger might project the roots of this dividedness as far back as Plato, when reason turned somewhat aggressive toward nature, but Plato's mythic genius kept reason and imagination fairly well together, natural symbols still giving rise to healthy thoughts. However, rather than trying to fix blame for the developments that have alienated us from nature, we probably do better to see them as virtually necessary steps in an evolutionary process. Immersed in what Voegelin has called the cosmological myth, even such advanced civilizations as the classical Mesopotamian did not differentiate divinity or the human spirit from the cosmological whole.[9] To gain the insights of the Greeks into the order of the human mind, or the insights of the Israelites into the divine transcendence, humanity had to break the cosmological myth. No longer could it run nature, society, divinity and the self together into one consubstantial whole.

The break brought an energizing but ambiguous sense of standing in a new era. It was exciting to have advanced humanity's sense of order and history a giant step, but also highly daunting. One could not go back, because regression would have meant the bad faith of denying a manifest truth, yet leaving the old cosmic home occasioned many a poignant nostalgia. Today the twenty-five hundred years of increasing alienation can seem an enormous derailment, especially to the intelligentsia who have to face the sufferings the differentiations have enabled. From the perspective of humanity's overall history, however, twenty-five hundred years are exceedingly brief, perhaps one two-hundredth of *homo sapiens'* total time. In a lifetime of eighty years, that would be about five months.

Still, they have been a momentous time, like the onset of puberty, when one races from childhood to the edge of maturity. Leaving the immediacies of childhood behind, the great intellectual seers grasped the mediating powers of reason, which proved isomorphic to the intelligibilities of nature, while the great affective seers grasped the redemptive powers of suffering love, which proved stronger than the cosmos' evils. The task today is so to apply what the great seers have learned that we bring reason and love to a new intimacy with nature. For this we need a new cosmological myth, a new rhapsodizing of nature's sacrality.

As the psychologists and anthropologists teach, powerful myths are not coolly manufactured. Madison Avenue has lightweight models, but the deep stories capable of uniting a people among themselves or with nature only well up from the recesses of the psyche, the fine point of the mystical soul. Laying hold of ancient and primordial symbols, such stories weld emotion, group contagion, reason, and love into dramas utterly persuasive, dances ushering into *mana,* the ultimate, incontrovertible power. The mammoth struggle through the human journey has been to see this power and live in reasonable, sanctifying ways. Those who plunge into *mana* irrationally, uncritically, with only raw enthusiasm usually emerge deranged or criminal. Those who hold back, from ignorance or fear, remain arid, spiritual dwarfs. The middle, balanced way is sharp as a razor, excruciatingly hard to discover. The few who do discover it emerge bloodied and scarred, like Jesus abandoned on Golgotha or the Buddha emaciated by fasting.

Still, because a few heroes like Jesus and the Buddha have ventured and won, the way to a new intimacy with nature is clear. Rational and balanced, it need neither deny God's transcendence of creation nor stand off from creation in shriveled alienation. Doing the things for our ecological peace, we can reconnect our ties to the cosmic rhythms, recharge our receptors of nature's sacrality, regenerate stories that help us choose life.[10] For Christians, this means a new mystagogy, with new sermons and rites. It means wax, water, and wine again instinct with the Spirit, filled with pneumatic power. It means making Christ the sacrament of nature's creator.

Chapter Nine:
ETHICAL IMPLICATIONS[1]

Preservation

Our final two chapters are practical, exercises in what Lonergan calls *communications*. Having imagined how the central notions of a new Christian theology of nature might best cohere, we turn to the policies that might honor nature's great value through effective actions.

The first policy is preservation. Until we realize that we are in sight of destroying nature and make a firm commitment to preserving nature in a healthy state, we have not begun to address the ecological crisis responsibly. Many of our current military and economic policies do not favor nature's preservation. Both globally and in the United States, nature is under heavy assault. The pollution that we documented in Part One, the acid rain and toxic wastes, is a mounting danger to nature's preservation. Great as the recuperative powers of the seas or the land may be, our present assumption that we can dump and erode at will is the height of ecological folly. We don't know enough about the different interlocking ecosystems to be sure that we won't soon reach a point of no return. We can no longer subject nature to our carelessness and greed without risking many species' futures.

At the beginning of a Christian natural ethics, then, stands a firm commitment to nature's preservation. Since we did not make material creation, we do not have the right to destroy material creation. At best God has placed nature in our care, made nature subject to our responsible stewardship. When we escalate the chances for nuclear war, expose the seas to widespread oil spillage, or countenance the rapid development of wilderness areas and jungles, we fail a God-given trust. Nature does not exist simply for our good pleasure. The mystery of nature's being, the Christology of nature's intelligibility, the occurrence of nature in God, and nature's impersonal revelations of God all argue that nature has a right to be, a right to live, a right to flourish apart from its utilities to human beings.

That is the heart of the ethical matter. Nature has an independent right to exist, live, and flourish. It is true that honoring this right is to our human advantage, since apart from a flourishing nature our human lives are greatly diminished. But our human advantage is not the prime consideration. Against the anthropocentrism that would make nature completely the servant of human well-being, a Christian theology of nature viable in the future will have to make a cosmocentric or theocentric stand. Either by fitting human beings into the grander scheme of natural history, or by fitting human beings into the ultimate scheme of the divine creation, it will have to demand that we become altruistic toward nature, start to take nature's well-being seriously into account. As a good guardian of a child has great concern for the welfare of his charge, so would a good steward of nature. As a good guardian considers all who threaten the welfare of his charge his enemies, so would a good steward of nature.

I do not mean, of course, that trees and human beings are equal. I am not saying that nature's rights to exist, live, and flourish are identical with those of a man or woman, or even those of a fetus in the womb. The proper relationship between nature and humanity admits of nature's serving many human needs. In few cases, however, should nature have to sacrifice being, life, or long-term flourishing. When the relationship between nature and humanity is sound, humanity usually will be able to replenish the natural resources it takes. Thus an ethics centered on preserving nature correlates with stresses on conservation, steady-state economics, and replenishing renewable resources. It opposes consumerism, an economics of constant growth, and the wasteful use of any resources. In today's crunch, these injurious attitudes manifest a vicious anthropocentrism, a sinful exaltation of human interests above those of other species, and also above those of God.

To be sure, there are also social reasons for urging the prosperous industrial nations to change their consumerist life-styles. High among such social reasons is the demand of distributive justice that we remove the glaring inequalities among the world's peoples' standards of living. But the ecological imperative to simplification is more potent than most ethicians have realized. If we are to preserve the earth, we have to change our gluttonous ways.

Seldom have I heard this imperative preached from a Christian pulpit. The priests and ministers who tell their people that high living is now a crime against nature are few and far between. Yet since Kant we've had the doughty precept that we should act so that our rationale might become universal law. An action whose rationale could not apply generally was by that fact immoral. Kant's precept applies today with shocking force. If I cannot extrapolate my standard of living to the whole world and still find nature flourishing, my standard of living is immoral.

So in addition to the traditional precept of Christian social ethics that I have no right to superfluities while other human beings lack necessities, the current state of nature makes it clear that I also have no right to luxuries whose general possession would bring nature to its knees. Most citizens of the United States seem to be violating this ecological precept. Apart from the people below the poverty line, the populace at large seems deeply guilty. If extended worldwide, our consumption of energy and our production of pollution would put the knife to nature's throat. Since we are no privileged race holding special exemption from nature's creator, we stand guilty and called to repentance. The first step in any repentance worthy of the name is committing ourselves to nature's preservation.

Future Generations

For whom are we to preserve nature? For God, for nature's own sake, and for the human generations to come. When we labor to preserve the creation God has poured forth, we affirm the sacred value of God's diffusion of his being. When we restrain our consumerism so that nature again may flourish, we pay homage to the impersonal facets of divinity shining forth from nature's whole. And when we foreswear our foolish short-sightedness, adopting economic policies that honor the long view, we bequeath our posterity a chance to be fully human, as our ancestors bequeathed that chance to us. Let us ponder this last implication of a sound ecological policy.

Preserving nature is a key part of a far-reaching vote for life. The two ways set before us each day, of death and life, insist that we exercise our enfranchisement. God has given us a say in nature's future; not to choose to make this say is to choose to join the nay-sayers. But when we join the nay-sayers, whether loudly or in silence, we join a conspiracy against our progeny, a conspiracy against our own flesh. If Erik Erikson has understood the life cycle correctly, we fail in the prime responsibility of our middle years.[2] From the time of adulthood, when we can procreate and serve the common good, we have an inbuilt need to be needed, an inbuilt need to generate. Physically and spiritually, our mature powers press for productivity, stewardship, and service. Ecological irresponsibility runs afoul of this generative pressure, setting up a dozen serious conflicts.

In large part, the problem is a failure of imagination, as the problem so frequently is. "What has posterity ever done for me?" we ask, compounding our lack of imagination with a patent selfishness.[3] Actually, posterity has always done a great deal for human adulthood. In many cultures it has furnished the main hopes for immortality, and in all cultures it has helped to set a horizon justifying sacrifice. Expecting that their progeny would profit from their sacrifices and hard work, people in many places and times have left home and emigrated. They have learned new languages, put up with low status, and hoped that their line one day would benefit. In

East Asia clan lines were so significant that Western observers misread their retrospective aspect as ancestor worship. In all parts of the globe the main value of marriage, traditionally, has not been the spouses' personal fulfillment but the procreation that would benefit the tribe.

Whatever changes the present population crisis and the present personalism force us to make in these millennial traditions, they do not remove the importance of our future generations. If our imaginations have so atrophied that we cannot picture our children's children's children, we are of all the generations of human history the most to be pitied. If our hope has so dwindled that we don't expect God to save our kind to the year 2100, we are of all the Christian generations the most in need of the parousia.

The fact is, our recent despoilation of nature relates intimately to our current shrinkage of hope. It is largely because we have put the world in nuclear and ecological bondage that we despair of a future humanity. Were we still friendly with nature, still deserving of the comforts nature's seemingly timeless cycles have always borne, we would not be so hopeless. We still can have God, the absolute future,[4] but few of us seem able to bear the naked faith in which a real God would give us a posterity. Without a solid fundament in a nature constantly witnessing to endurance, we mainly constrict our vision to today. Lifting up our eyes to hills no longer everlasting, we find no whence from which our hope might come.

If we want to be ethical, we must confess our pusillanimity and start to turn things around. Acknowledging that our present ecological policies have cast posterity in the shade, we must reject these policies and fashion new ones full of hope. The rational response to the judgment that a given level of consumption imperils the future of nature or our posterity is to lower that level of consumption. The rational response to the judgment that a given level of population growth imperils the future of nature or our posterity is to lower that level of population growth. We have made some progress on population growth, though not enough to secure the future or proclaim ourselves rational. We have made very little progress on consumption, largely because our politics pivot on greed and our religion pivots on comfort.

Our politics pivot on greed, in that nearly all our candidates for office stand on a platform of protecting our materialist good life economically and militarily. Our religion pivots on comfort, in that nearly all our pastors keep their sermons far from the bank accounts or luxuries of their lowing flocks. If the scenarios of the environmentalists are warranted, as I believe any objective analysis shows them to be, a rational politics or religion would straightforwardly calculate the global levels of consumption supportable in the future, imagine how most fairly to distribute the sacrifices needed to meet those levels, and set to the work of shifting the culture at large from a base in relatively gross material satisfactions to a base in spiritual satisfactions immeasurably more human. But it takes courage to be rational, as the barest of human experience shows, and neither our politicians nor our clergy presently stand out for courage. Until they do, posterity will be an endangered species.

Carrying Capacity

In calculating the global levels of consumption supportable in the future, a key index is the earth's overall *carrying capacity* ("The maximum population size that a given ecosystem can support indefinitely under a given set of environmental conditions is called the ecosystem's *carrying capacity*").[5] This concept alone does not specify the whole conservationist or preservationist task, but it takes a big bite out of the central problem. Were an ethics seriously to focus on the ingredients and consequences of establishing such a crucial policy goal as tailoring the nations' future economies to a reasonable global carrying capacity, it would soon find its practical problems and targets clarifying so concretely that there would be a heavy run on its bank of courage. I assume that the ethical portion of a Christian theology of nature viable in the future will want to employ such rational tools as carrying capacity, and that it will want to buttress with Christian ideals the practical actions such tools project. Let us meditate briefly on what such a buttressing-process might entail.

Suppose that the state of the demographic art were to establish the earth's carrying capacity at six billion human beings. I take this figure simply for illustration. Agriculturalists, economists, nutritionists, and other relevant experts would have made their best calculations, put their heads together, and come up with, "Voila! Six billion." The reasonable person, having studied these experts' assumptions, data, and inferences and concluded that they seemed sound, would stand ready to accept the practical consequences: How do we set our sights on this optimal figure? How do we generate the food production, the distribution of goods, the medical and cultural regimes that the imagined lives of these six billion seem to call for?

What would the person of lively Christian faith likely add? First, she likely would add a sanction for rationality itself, perhaps based on a fresh interpretation of Genesis 1:28 ("Be fruitful and multiply, and fill the earth and subdue it"). To execute today the role of stewards in which God has placed us, we have to use our minds and discipline our wills, determining the common good and dedicating ourselves to its realization. As ecological studies have dramatically shown, the human factor in natural history is now crucial, all too often even lethal. The way that we are intervening in nature is changing nature dramatically, sometimes for the good, all too often for nature's ruin.

The greenhouse effect, for instance, is throwing brackets around many of the next century's natural patterns. Our energy use has slowly been raising the temperature of the atmosphere, to the point where weather patterns may be changing and the polar ices may soon begin to melt. No one can predict with certainty all the effects of such melting, especially in coastal areas, nor of such related effects as the destruction of the ozone screen that presently shields us against solar radiation.

If we are to carry out the intent that an enviromentally sensitive theology finds in Genesis 1:28, the intent of the creator that we live gracefully and symbiotically with nature, not twisting nature out of shape by our greed, we have to make faith the champion of policies (such as trying to reverse the greenhouse effect) that activate our best estimates of what the survival and prosperity of the total ecosystem demand. Any pitting of faith against this sort of reason would be counterproductive to a good creator's likely intent and rightly would earn the contempt of the people laboring most rationally and generously for the earth's preservation.

Unfortunately, this conflict between Christian faith and reason is not idle speculation. The alliance of certain Christians with exploitative capitalism, the veneer of religion painted over making money in many business successes, can produce a line of "ugly Christians," come into the natural and social world to rape and begrime. Therefore we need a clarion call, from all Christians with the brains to grasp and the lungs to yell, to the countereffect that God's way is toward reason, common sense, survival, and sacrifice, that making money is not on the list of the Christian virtues. Indeed, money stands high on the list of worldly entities that Christianity holds deeply suspect, because more times than not affluence comes through serious injustice.

Today the facts of our social and natural history make a strong case that the energetic promotion of trivial luxuries such as cosmetics, to say nothing of symbolizing high human achievement as a pink Cadillac, is irresponsible to the point of gross objective sin. God may be forgiving our powder-puff pirates, as he may be forgiving our pirates of oil or real estate, because many of them appear so stunted that they know not what they do, but objectively they are minions of Beelzebub.

Second, the person of lively Christian faith probably would move beyond supporting what is rational to soliciting what is loving, generously self-sacrificing. As 1 John saw long ago, one cannot claim to love God and close his heart to a fellow-human in need (3:17). Today the Christian ethician of nature can infer that one cannot claim to love God and aid the destruction of God's creation. Today the charity of Christ that urges us to sacrifice for our fellow-human beings also urges us to cut back on our consumption, sacrifice our luxuries, and give up our pollution for the sake of nature's preservation. Today the promise of a hundredfold now and heaven hereafter (Mark 10:30) must apply to ecological sacrifices, so important have they become to creation's future.

Population Control

Any realistic assessment of the earth's carrying capacity is going to imply that we human beings have to put stern controls on our population growth. Moreover, we have to put these controls on quickly, because time is running out. As Carl Djerassi expressed it at the end of his two-volume work, *The Politics of Contraception:* "In birth control, time is *the* most expensive commodity. Every day 350,000 babies are born in this world but only 200,000 persons die. Yet we act as if we had an unlimited amount of time. We do not, which is why I have written this book."[6]

The simplest use of Djerassi's figures shows that we gain at least 150,000 people per day, at least a million people per week, at least fifty million people per year. Let the population of the world in 1980 have been four billion and by the year 2020 the world probably will have at least six billion people. In 1800 the world had about 900 million people. In 1900 it had about 1.6 billion people. The two hundred years + from 1800 to 2020 therefore likely will show a population increase of 667 percent. The one hundred years + from 1900 to 2020 likely will show an increase of 375 percent. Those are rates we simply cannot sustain. Were we to survive to the year 2100, maintaining the 375 percent rate of increase that obtained from 1900 to 2020, we would have a world population of about 20 billion. All sorts of factors could deflect us from such growth, but the basic numbers, the statistical inertia, are bearing down on such a target ominously.

This statistical inertia has persuaded many conservationists that we need to target a goal of zero population growth (zpg). Already we have so many people in the world that food, health, education, and employment are crushing problems.

Moreover, the problems are not evenly distributed, because our subpopulations neither consume resources nor reproduce themselves at the same rates. The bulges in the population cycles occur among the world's poorest peoples, whose reproduction rates are quite high. The world's wealthier peoples have imposed stronger birth controls on themselves, but the average person in a wealthy nation uses many more natural resources than the average person in a poor nation. (The ratio of the consumption of the average American to that of the average Indian is perhaps 6:1.) So we need population control all along the economic spectrum: at the wealthy end, to put a brake on the consumption of natural resources; at the poor end, to stop the population explosion and the critical shortages of food, medicine, and the like; in the middle, simply to keep the total population down. To reach zpg, we need an overall reduction in the birthrate of about 43% (150,000/350,000).

An especially grim byproduct of the population crisis is a cancerous urbanization. In 1900 the vast majority of the world's people lived in the country. In 1980 about 39 percent lived in cities and towns. "If present trends continue, by the close of this century at least half of the people in the world will live in urban areas, with perhaps half of these people unemployed or unable to earn a living wage. To accommodate these new urban dwellers, between 1980 and 2000 the world will need housing, utilities, schools, hospitals, and commercial enterprises equivalent to building 1,600 cities of a million people each—an average of 80 such cities each year. This does not even include the rebuilding and revitalizing of today's cities."[7]

Another way of dramatizing the extent of urbanization is to report the demographers' predictions of the sizes that various cities will have attained by the year 2000. Mexico City likely will have grown to 31 million, Tokyo to 24 million, Shanghai to 23 million, São Paulo to 21 million, and New York to 21 million. Already we wonder whether these cities are fit for human habitation. Already their crime, bad housing, sanitation problems, unemployment, and general level of tension make us wonder whether we are creating a terrible strain of mutants, like locusts spawned from crickets whose

141

population has become too dense. The conditions likely to obtain in a Mexico City of 31 million beggar the imagination and suck away the spirit.

The ethical imperative couched in these population figures is no mystery. We can reduce it to a single word: STOP! There is room for legitimate debate about the best means to achieve something close to zpg, but there is no room or time for debate about the necessity of zpg itself. If future generations are to have the right to a life worth designating human, their numbers must tally to a reasonable sum. The present demographic trends make any moves toward a redistribution of world's riches sadly quixotic, and they practically guarantee decades and decades of military confrontation.

Christian spokespersons have an important role to play in making zpg persuasive, but to date their message has been blurred. Some have stood in the forefront of planned parenthood, while others (unfortunately those with most influence in the areas of most rapid population growth) have lost sight of the big question and nitpicked about the morality of mechanical and chemical contraceptives. Such "natural" methods as studying the body's temperature changes to determine the time of ovulation may prove very helpful, but we won't have a vigorous ethical response from Christians until their leaders have knocked over many remaining taboos. Then the socioeconomic barriers to population control will stand out more clearly, reminding us that until third world people feel secure enough not to need an army of sons and daughters, the population crisis will continue to tick away like a megaton bomb.

Genuine Need[8]

We have been speaking of a Christian naturalist ethics that would stress preservation, future generations, the globe's carrying capacity, and population control. These are rational emphases that a fair reading of the ecological facts should promote. Buttressed by Christian faith in nature's great value, they could greatly change the way we treat the material world. An emphasis equally necessary and more demanding is reducing human beings' demands upon the ecosystem to those that result from genuine needs. Perhaps this is the policy most in need of Christian support. If so, a Christian naturalist ethics viable in the future probably will have to equate the good life with the simple life, the life of few material wants.

The earth most likely could support six billion human beings, were they to live simple lives of few material wants. Nature probably is more than bountiful enough to carry this load. Assuming that the few material wants were not highly polluting, and that we greatly reduced our assault on the earth's non-renewable resources, the six billion human beings would have a good chance of establishing a self-sustaining, steady-state economy. If they went on to redistribute the world's riches, so that all people had roughly the same share, they would defuse the main social disorder threatening the world's survival. Then an ecologically sound society might arise, able to concentrate on the creative technology, science, religion, art, and social services at the center of a rich cultural life. A few people would have to sacrifice some material comforts, but a great many more people would have the chance to gain great spiritual enrichment.

This is a utopian dream, far from the pragmatic scenarios on most politicians' desks, but it can be quite instructive for Christian spirituality, as I hope to show in the next chapter. Here the main point remains more pedestrian: how to reduce the world's consumption so as to make a reasonable carrying capacity viable. With land and mineral resources strictly limited, human beings have to start using only what they genuinely need. Since the world's most profligate users, the people of the Northern industrial nations, likely will hear a call to consume only what they genuinely need as a harsh demand for sacrifice, and since the major religious resource in these Northern industrial nations continues to be the Christian churches, a special burden falls upon Christian ethicians. Unless they clarify the moral task before the Northern nations and make it bearable, a viable carrying capacity or steady-state economy will remain a chimera.

The moral task is easily sketched. We have to leave our

over-concern with material pleasures, gadgets, luxuries, and distractions, and get back to the basics, the perennial roots of a rich personal and social life. Our preachers, theologians, ethicians, novelists, and other putative seers have to show us the visions that will gild this turn-about, this conversion, with the gold of God's grace. Only if changing our present lifestyle seems a great opportunity to grow will it have any significant chance of taking hold. Moral exhortation alone moves only the few. The many must feel they are starting an adventure, setting out on a more excellent way.

Fortunately, they definitely would be. Shifting to an economy and culture based on genuine needs rather than superfluities would enhance the lives of most people in the developed nations. For example, in the United States Johnny might learn how to read, Johnny's dad might not have a coronary at fifty, Johnny's mom might not weigh two hundred pounds, and Johnny's little sister might enter a society of sexual equality. Today too many Johnnys are functionally illiterate, barely able to grunt and scratch. Too many parents labor in boring jobs, too many citizens of all ages mope for want of hard exercise and a sound diet, and too many women paid 59¢ to every male $1.00 are expected to furnish society 75% of its comfort and beauty. Yet consumerism is so central to our current American culture that shifting to an economics of genuine needs would open the door to changes in these and a dozen other central areas.

It's hard to imagine the United States making these changes, shifting from a consumerist ethic to an ethic stressing genuine needs. That would be like a junkie going cold turkey, an alcoholic staying on the wagon. As in those cases, however, the pain of an abusive lifestyle would be a major ally in the conversion process. When the junkie realizes that he will die, probably in prison, unless he breaks his destructive habit, he may be able to muster the courage to quit. The same with the alcoholic. At his wit's end, reduced to his final shreds of dignity, he may finally be able to confess his utter misery and seek the help he needs. In neither case would one wish their pains upon these terrible sufferers. However, if pain be the only way to save their lives, let pain run down like a rushing stream.

Similarly, no one but a sadist would wish upon the United States the unemployment, worry, trivialization, greed, and disappointment that the misconceived American dream now is bringing, yet this suffering is a great opportunity. Millions have bought a terrible bill of goods, star-studded with the premise that money and possessions will make them happy. The dream was bound to turn nightmarish. Had we listened to Buddha, Lao Tzu, Plato, or Jesus, we would have known the end would be sad. Only a strong spirit gives rich humanity. The only good life is that which supplies our material necessities (food, shelter, medical care) and encourages our spirits to soar in art, science, healing, prayer, and other creative ventures.

Appropriate Technology

Were we to stress population control and reducing human needs to those truly necessary, we would be on the way to answering two of the main questions interposing themselves between humanity and a happy year 2100. There still would remain, however, serious questions about our present technological system and about our present preoccupation with making (or preparing for) war. Let us defer the problem of war to the next chapter, where we will be reflecting on non-violence and reconciliation. That leaves the question of technology.[9]

The main problems with our current technological system include the fact that it seems to run us more than we run it, and the fact that frequently it treats nature destructively. Along with the military establishments, the industrial complexes of the Northern nations are the strongest determiners of the Northern economies, if not of the entire Northern cultures. In less than a full generation, military hardware, computer hardware and software, and energy technologies have changed our political, mental, and physical landscapes dramatically. The genius of "how to do," in the sense of how to change, calculate, and control, stands out as the great logo of our age. What should naturalist ethicians make of this emblematic genius, in the context of mapping the moral strategies necessary for a fair ecological future?

Many of the technologies themselves are indifferent, with the large exception of the military technologies. Only if one can justify nuclear war as a moral means of self-defense can one justify nuclear weaponry or, analogously, the rockets, drones, chemical weapons, and other horrors the weapons industries steadily produce. If one considers manufacturing the means of the race's destruction to be madness, one will find few of our weapons systems morally justified. The argument that forces of evil threaten our survival or freedom and so require us to prepare to defend ourselves is theoretically impressive, but the actual determination of these forces of evil, and the many other economic and diplomatic alternatives that would have to be exhausted before taking military options seriously, put a great burden of proof on the ethician who would try to justify our current production of military technology.

The computer and energy technologies are more indifferent, yet still possessed of significant dangers. If we do not balance computer skills with traditional education in the sciences and the humanities, we produce peculiar human beings, brilliant in one dimension but incompetent morally, in matters that do more than count. Computer circuitry itself cannot answer the question of what uses computer technology should serve. We have to choose whether medical uses should bulk larger than military uses, whether to pay more attention to social security than to aviation or solar energy.

Ideally, technology should serve human needs. A rational policy would put the best technology at the service of society's greatest needs. It is a question of priorities. It is clear to me that today the greatest needs occur among the world's poor, whose lack of food, clothing, medicine, education, and the like makes their lives full of suffering. The fact that even third world economies put huge portions of their monies and resources toward military uses shows that almost all countries have caught the fever of irrationality. In part this is due to self-serving leaders, who want military might for the sake of international clout. In part it is due to the seductions of the developed countries, who woo any countries willing to pay them for weapons or computer technology.

E. F. Schumacher developed a rational alternative when he pioneered small, carefully tailored technologies that would serve the real needs of under-developed economies: producing enough food, shelter, and medicine to take care of their poverty-stricken populations. Schumacher showed that a little imagination, combined with a willingness to listen to local people's stories, could start to generate a new level of technology, which he called "intermediate," that often allowed native peoples greatly to increase their productivity without having to assemble great amounts of capital. If countries were able to get out of the vicious circle of simply supplying developed countries with raw materials and depending on developed countries for their finished products, they might be able to make good progress in solving their real problems.

There are many international programs run by the United Nations or church groups that deserve great praise for their efforts to help native people develop an appropriate technology. To date, however, the gigantic economies of the industrial nations have tended to dominate all the efforts of the industrially less developed. The developing nations usually lack both capital and know-how, so they must derive their technology from the Northern nations, whose advantage it is to keep the smaller nations in their debt. This self-service of the Northern nations, combined with the dawn of tomorrow's ecological crises, makes the development of a small-scale, appropriate technology especially compelling.

Chapter Ten:
IMPLICATIONS FOR SPIRITUALITY

Interrelatedness

Spirituality is where the individual Christian tries to put her convictions together and effectively obey Jesus' twofold command. What implications do the dialectical, foundational, doctrinal, systematic, and ethical aspects of a naturalist Christian theology seem to hold for our future Christian spirituality? How might the things we have seen of nature's great value, creation's powers to manifest God, and the pending ecological crises influence the Christian who is trying to love God with his whole mind, heart, soul, and strength, and trying to love his neighbor as himself? These are the sorts of questions we consider in this chapter.

Perhaps the first impact should come from the notion of ecology itself. As soon as one grasps the view of material creation that "ecology" imports, things no longer stand apart from one another. No citizen of material creation stands in splendid isolation, not even *homo sapiens,* Rodin's solitary thinker. As much as the other animals, we humans are convivial with the rest of nature, depending upon our fellow creatures for food, sustenance, and habitat. Make any serious changes in the material environment of a human tribe and you change that tribe's way of life drastically, perhaps even irreparably.

That was what anthropologist Colin Turnbull found among the Ik, a mountain tribe who used to wander between Kenya and Uganda. When they no longer could follow their old hunting routes and support themselves in their traditional ways, the Ik became disoriented, demoralized, barely human.[1]

Turnbull previously had found a similar, though more positive ecological dependency among the Pygmies of the (then Belgian) Congo. In their case the surrounding forest habitat was favoring, but the influence was just as great.[2]

We citizens of the Northern industrial nations may think ourselves indifferent to our natural environments, but we belie such pretense everyday. Not only do we continue to discriminate beach people from mountain people, those who stroll in the park from those who hike in the woods. We also talk almost obsessively about the weather, the view out the window, the return of our triennial wanderlust. Environment comes into the home in the person of the interior decorator, who daubs and drapes to create surroundings that will help us work well, make us feel better. Redoing her kitchen in classical French white, the California homemaker has visions of Julia Child, gourmet cuisine, a maison of deeper and deeper contentment. Tending her fragile plants in the sunspace, the novice horticulturalist prays to God to heal her black thumb: she needs the pickup, the color, the vitality of her green plants, pale grasses, shy little pansies.

One could take this line of reflection on international flights, comparing the gardens of Japan with the dusty paths of India, the breathtaking ride from Oslo to Bergen with a sail among the Greek islands. The people in any of those locales remain mysterious, for they all are more than what they see and eat, but we understand a great deal more about them for having breathed their air, heard their sounds, seen their sights. In important part, a people is the land it lives in, the environment with which daily it interacts. Any people is symbiotic with its atmosphere, its waterways, its hills, its valleys, its plains. Human beings have always known this instinctively, as their stubborn loyalties to even wretched homelands show. But the ecological sciences have made it possible for all of us to know it expressly, with greater precision, as a universal law of life.

All life is relational. The universe forms a system. Within the universe, various subsystems group inanimate and animate things into patterns of mutual influence. Pull on one of these things, and you move another. Make a change in the chemistry, biology, or nutrition of one partner to the system and you likely shift the system as a whole. If only through the smudge of our oil or the smell of our toxic gases, we have begun to realize how interdependent material creation is. It is now costly to think in isolationist terms, to ignore creation's connections. The task for spiritual theologians is to make interconnectedness desirable, beautiful, and sanctifying.

If I am to love God well in the ecological future, I need to expand my appreciation of God's creatorship. Until I realize that God is the ultimate force and present depth of the giant stars, the microscopic mites, the lilies and the otters, I miss most of the import of "creator." God is not only my God, the maker of the peoples of my tribe. God is also lord of the lion, the dolphin, the tiger burning bright. "Glory be to God for dappled things," Hopkins and others have exclaimed. For them the inscape, the most central form, of each and every being was a touch of the finger of God. Living in the midst of such a creation, they never lacked for psalms to sing. Interrelatedness was at the marrow of their spirituality, so they could love creation like a home. Perhaps they were so exceptional that we delude ourselves in thinking we can follow in their footsteps. Deluded or not, though, we can be certain that ecology invites us to try.

Naturalist Prayer

When we start to walk in the footsteps of the poets and naturalists who have most deeply appreciated material creation, we verge upon a naturalist prayer. Contemplating the beauty, or power, or connectedness of the world, we come to within a step of praising the world's creator. And even when our contemplations turn to stone, because they must deal with earthquakes, cancers, or other of nature's destructive powers, the problems of evil, disorder, and wreckage they raise can bring us heart to heart with God.

Further, if we have started to study the lessons of interconnectedness, we will not separate our ecological follies from our social. The food not distributed, the sicknesses not healed, and the brains allowed to atrophy all testify to the folly of our current economics, our current politics, our current ways of viewing the world. Energy is not an island, nor recreation, nor industrial production. When we choose to produce luxurious cars we choose to limit future human lives. When we strew the landscape with garbage, we taint another portion of our soul. Like a gaunt traditional guru, ecology says again and again: "Let the eye of your mind be simple, the will of your heart be pure," for where your disorder is, there will great pollution follow.

In a nervous and conflicted time, the therapies of a simple, naturalist contemplation can be quite important. At the office, in the study, pondering the newest tax laws, we find the world a hopeless tangle of precedents, decisions, vested interests. Looking out the bay window, standing before the sound, this man-made convolution drops away. Before the masterwork of God, our human contrivances seem awkward and inelegant. Consider the lilies of the field, how they grow. Consider the birds of the air. On only seed, soil, sunshine, and rain, the lilies outshine Cezanne. Neither toiling nor reaping, the birds outfly McDonnell-Douglas.

Contemplating these natural wonders, the Christian spirit may stress either the mystery of how they are so beautiful or the mystery that they are so hardy. The mystery of how they are beckons the mind of God, the providence of God, the original comprehensive act that envisioned all creatures' endless correlations. The mystery that they are beckons the primordial issue of being. Lilies and birds are, when easily they could not be. They are beautiful and persevering, when easily their enemies on one side or their frailties on the other could leave them slashed and marred.

Shiva, the Lord of the Dance of Life and Death, taught the Indian mind to keep being and non-being connected. Creation, Christianity's main symbol for the first beginnings, taught the Western mind to keep being connected with God. No matter that science distinguishes dozens of intermediate causes. Correct and useful as science is, it diminishes the ultimate wonder of the lilies of the field, the ultimate mystery of the birds of the air, less than a jot or a tittle. On the day we know all we can know about a lily or a sparrow, we still will not know why this lily came to be, what end this sparrow serves, whose good pleasure conceived these or any creatures with a grin.

To move from pondering lilies and sparrows to acts of Christian prayer, we need only lift mind and heart to the mystery at any creature's beginning, in any creature's depths, luring all beings to their term. God is this comprehensive mystery, near as the pulsebeat at our throats. We would not seek God had we not already found God. Our turn to God, our lifting of mind or heart, is but a response to God's prior grace. The spirit of these traditional theses gains a rich body of examples out in the fields, along the rivers, by the shore when the tide rushes in. Sunrise, sunset, easily the spirit can soar. If we but move our spirit toward the mystery, but let it linger in wordless appreciation, we pray a saving prayer. "God keep this beauty," we mumble. "God make this power go well." This day our souls may be required of us, we may have to rejoin the Great Clod. You know, God, that we are simply people, and our lives are short. We have never seen you. All we have are Jesus' face, a few good books, the handshake of our friends, and nature's steady consistency.

When possible, let us rest upon nature's constancy like a bosom, taking pleasure, nurture, and repose. Nature has always been the Great Mother: consort of Father Sky, context of titanic culture, for thousands of years our primal visage. Friend and foe, she has chased us down the nights and up the days, hounding us to grow mystic. Because seed fell in nature's ground and rose again months after, people began to think they might rise again, on Spring days they later called Easter. Because the sun rose in the East, set in the West, and rose again in the East the next day, the Egyptians thought a golden god traveled the sky by day and trudged the underworld by night, dragging his barge across sand. Who is to say the Egyptians did not capture life before the parousia? If we paid more attention to the sun in prayer, and less attention to the sun in war, we'd have higher hopes of greeting the sun of justice today and all days, unto ages of ages. That could come from an orthodox naturalism, a prayer at home in God's world. Made catholic, set in protest against all the prayerless regimes driving us against nature like an enemy, it could mount a great counterforce for peace.

Non-Violence[3]

In the last chapter I mentioned the capital problem of war-making, its technological and economic clout. Clearly nuclear war is now the greatest threat to the nations' survival, and the greatest drain on the nations' economies. Contemplating nuclear war, we all are drawn to the brink of hopelessness. Analyzing the costs of preparing for nuclear war, we realize why a dozen clusters of social needs go unattended. There is now no greater monument to human folly than the nuclear impasse we've created. Factories whirr, planes patrol, submarines prowl the deep, because the nations and their leaders cannot bring themselves to secure the peace. For the profit, pride, and paranoia in it, the nations and their leaders prefer to keep building arms. They have so little imagination they can prattle mindlessly about life after the holocaust, so little wit they cannot see the hangman's noose around the next generation's neck.

The ultimate threat of nuclear war is that it would destroy the earth's carrying capacity, abort the millennial evolutionary process. That might not happen, but then again it might. Who can say for sure? And who, not being able to say for sure, rationally would take a step closer to possessing the capacity to destroy the earth's ecosphere? Perhaps that would be the ultimate impiety and sacrilege: to cause creation to die. When human beings kill one another, they bluster about injustice, territorial expansion, or some other pseudo-justification of their bloodlust. The same occurs when they abort their fetuses, though there the tale often is sadder. But what rationalization shall we confect to cover our death-blows against creation itself? How shall we tell history, which of course will be no more, relegated only to God's memory, that our nuclear weapons, or chemical weapons, or genetic manipulations, or computer technologies go so out of hand they turned against the whole of earthly creation?

Rebounding from this worst-case scenario (which, unfortunately, is by no means impossible), let us see clearly the alternative we need, if we are to walk away from the impending doomsday. The alternative is non-violence, what the Indians have long called *ahimsa*. So long as we act violently, abusively, injuriously, we will continue to career down the highway to disaster. If we begin to tame our violence, exorcise our demonic destructiveness, develop attitudes of construction and connection, we may find we still have a chance.

Non-violence obviously can apply at many levels, and we need to contemplate as many of these levels as we can. Most universally, the current arms race and engines of ecological pollution are the most violent threats to the earth's survival. Scarcely below them ranks the violence the nations inflict on one another, especially the systemic *violencia blanca* encoded in the current economic arrangements. On the personal level, each of us could profit from an examination of conscience, to see whether our work, family life, or religion is sufficiently averted from warmaking and conflict to merit Jesus' praise, sufficiently turned toward reconciliation and peace.

As the Taoists acutely realized, many of nature's own ways are indirect and non-violent. Take a great, forbidding rock. Let it thrust forth into the sea, like the sword of an imperial commander. Slowly, patiently, irresistibly, the sea will wear this rock down. Nature often goes softly, slowly, by degrees. Often it shows a mute faith in the ways of its creator, a trust that its next season will come round. Many of the most intense religious regimes have been driven by a conviction that there are natural wisdoms culture has been covering over: the wisdom to hear our bodies, and so to feed, clothe, and work them well; the wisdom to fit into nature harmoniously: prizing a beautiful environment, putting a high price-tag on quiet and peace; the wisdom to find nature a revelation of meaning, not just another parcel to exploit.

For the individual Christian trying to develop an ecological spirituality, the key to most external acts of non-violence more and more will be seen to lie within. When we gain the respect for nature that God's presence should give it, and gain in ourselves the contentment that conversion can bring, we will be poised to begin treating all our fellow creatures gratefully, gently, as though we bore them much love.

The twofold command that epitomizes Jesus' teaching, the love of God totally and love of neighbor as ourselves, holds today this ecological implication. When we begin to treat nature like ourselves, with respect and gentleness, we will not only love God in his natural form, we will also dramatically extend the implication of "neighbor." Presently a great deal of our global trauma comes from the energies we pour into misdirected, destructive, hostile channels. Feminists have stigmatized much of this craziness as machismo, and their stigma has great merit. But few of us are wholly innocent of abusive actions, or of attitudes that tend to our neighbors' ruin. Few of us are so converted to God that we bless all the beauty we see and reach to give the shirt from our backs. In the future, these virtues may not be a luxury. In the future, non-violence and gentleness may be our only ways to survival.

Reconciliation

If *ahimsa* is the traditional word that the Indian religions offer an ecological spirituality, the traditional Christian word is *reconciliation*. And whereas in biblical times the main significance of reconciliation was breaking down barriers among human beings, today reconciliation has to include breaking down barriers between human beings and nature. So alienated from nature have many sectors of the industrial nations become that a real enmity has developed. Nature has turned sour and destructive, because of the abuse steadily heaped upon it. Where once there was a strong hope that earth might be fair and all her children wise, a sullen grime now mars earth's face and most of her children seem foolish. Any spiri-

155

tuality in tune with tomorrow's needs will want to be sure that it works on the side of the angels of ecological reconciliation.

Some such angels of ecological reconciliation are organic farming, solar energy, and sound housing construction, all of which reduce the intrusions we make into nature. The reclamation projects under way in many parts of the globe and many sectors of the economy offer another strong beam of hope. Barbara Ward has an informative paragraph on the recycling of paper which, if read between the lines, summarizes the core problems in ecological reconciliation: "Inevitably, the degree to which governments have succeeded in encouraging a new mood of thrift is still uncertain. Both consumers and the productive sector have far too many varied interests for any set of regulations or costs to have anything like uniform effects. Take, for instance, the general conflict between the producers of original raw materials and those who wish to substitute recycled residues. There is likely to be a strong logging lobby anxious to avoid too large an expansion in the use of recycled paper. An estimated 300 million trees a year could be saved in the United States through tripling the amount of paper recycled, but very likely some loss of work and profit for the pulp industry would be entailed. Paper companies tend to turn to the recycled material only to cover temporary shortages or surges of demand. The result is alternating glut and famine for second-hand paper dealers and often complete discouragement for civic-minded groups collecting the paper for the public good."[4]

This simple example shows several places where reconciliation seems needed. First, there is the general problem of getting people to realize that their present, wasteful attitudes toward nature are moving their societies in the wrong direction. These people need to be reconciled to a new, ecological outlook, in which waste is cut and recycling becomes a standard policy. Second, there are the many particular problems that any economic shift is likely to entail. In this case, society needs intermediaries who will ease the burdens on the loggers and the second-hand paper dealers that a new policy of paper recycling might create. A serious implication of shifts as far-going as many that ecological conversion would promote is that society at large has to shoulder the burdens that individuals suffer because of policy changes targeted for the common good. Too often we slip by this implication, not being as willing to ask the overall populace to pay the costs of the benefits they will receive as we are eager to paint those benefits in glowing terms. This does not mean that major contributors to ecological problems should not have to pay a major part of the tariff. The short-sightedness and greed of the automobile companies, for example, has been a significant factor in the rise of our energy and air pollution crises, so it is right that the automobile companies help pay to resolve them. But the automobile companies have had considerable support from a luxury-seeking, head-in-the-sand American public, so they should not have to bear the costs of clean air alone.

The rest of Ward's paragraph offers the comfort that problems of recycling and reconciliation are not limited to the United States: "In 1974, both the French and the British authorities found themselves all but buried under mounds of unwanted used paper. It is for this reason that a number of governments, including the French, the Japanese, and the Norwegian, are setting up orderly guaranteed markets for recycled paper through such measures as subsidized collecting centers, storage space, and guaranteed prices. If the next step is to tax the original timber, then the real conflict with logging interests begins. Nor is the dilemma confined to wood and pulp. In the United States, for instance, depletion allowances and special transport rates give a strong economic advantage to the use of virgin ores. In a world of increasing resource shortages, the policy makes no sense at all."[5]

Again and again one comes across that phrase: the policy makes no sense at all. To anyone devoted to world peace, ecological restoration, and social justice, reason seems in most governments to have gone on holiday. Worse, often reason seems to have been tossed out of all serious consideration, tossed into chains and locked in the dungeon. Beholden to a big business which unabashedly serves the great god financial profit, and cowed by the general public's unconcern for the future, the recent American governments haven't had the imagination or backbone of a woolly caterpillar. At the deepest levels, then, an ecological spirituality has first to reconcile the Christian to his people's sin: the aversion from the reasonable God that is pitting his country to the core.

Hope

One of the best features of Barbara Ward's *Progress for a Small Planet* is the passel of positive examples it offers. On dozens of ecological problems, in dozens of countries all over the world, people have made striking progress and really turned things around. There *are* solutions to many of our problems, if we are able politically to take them. We have the understanding necessary to live harmoniously with nature; our will is what is questionable. All four partners to the ecological crisis—nature, society, the self, and God—offer solid grounds for hope. Nature is forgiving, in the sense that when we stop abusing her systems, usually she starts returning to health. Many societies have on occasion developed and executed enlightened policies, offering us a large number of precedents. The self always is free to develop an ecological spirituality (no one can force you to be wasteful). God has given us both a marvelous creation and marvelous minds with which to understand it. The choice therefore is our own. If nature ends up polluted, or the world ends up malnourished, or the nations push one another into war, we will have only ourselves to blame.

For me this is sufficient grounds for hope. So long as I find solutions possible, the sun shines enough to light my way, the storms are secondary. Perhaps this is a function of my theology of grace, and worth making explicit. So many people reject my hope, finding its bases too thin, that it might be well to uncover the connections between their different assumptions about human nature and their different theologies of grace.

I assume that human nature is weak and wounded, but not essentially corrupted. I assume that reason still has a firm appeal to the strong character, a vestigial appeal even to the weak. The roots of this anthropology lie deep in my faith. I take seriously the Pauline proclamation that where sin abounded grace abounds the more. I take equally seriously the Johannine reflection that the light has shone in the world and the darkness has not overcome it. In creating the world, God made a beautiful place resonant with the unlimited resources of the Father, coruscant with the full intelligibility of the Logos, instinct with the healing love of the Holy Spirit. In incarnating the Son, God drew as close to the material world as he could, uniting his expression to one of his creatures. In redeeming the world by the blood of Christ's cross, God showed the farthest reaches of the divine love: even though the reasoning species of the world had turned away, God continued to be loving, finally proving that love is stronger than death.

Concretized, these theologoumena mean that the forces I call ultimate are all on our side. How they come to our aid is mysterious, but I cannot deny that they come without forfeiting my Christian allegiance. So, for example, in contemplating a progressive ecological proposal, I have to believe that God supports the sweet reason, reconciliation, and non-violence it carries. Having studied causes such as building passive solar houses, recycling paper, and scrubbing smokestacks to reduce dirty emissions, I have to think that they are the wave of the future. The resistance they encounter is distressing, but ultimately not the point. So long as good minds and hearts continue to propose solid solutions, the light is still shining in the darkness. Like the widow before the unjust judge, our job is to keep nagging, keep arguing, keep refusing to let the bastards wear us down. Bastards they are, spawn of stupidity and greed. There is no need to sugarcoat their likely bloodlines. But their positions carry the seeds of their own overthrowing, so the worst thing we could do would be to take up the fight on their terms.

That is the danger to which a pessimistic anthropology always is liable. Lacking a solid theology of grace, it is tempted to forget that the light is shining in the darkness, that sin is never the equal of grace. Those commentators from the American past or present who speak about human nature as though it were bound to be corrupt, as though we could never elicit a citizenry reasonable and generous, are a major part of our ecological problem. Filling the airwaves with self-fulfilling prophecies, they predict the omnipresence of prodigals and then moan that their predictions have come true. Unfortunately, they are as rife in the churches as in the newspapers and legislatures, and the do-nothing establishment depends on their cynicism.

A contrary, Christian expression of hope (hope *is* one of the theological virtues, you recall) would go right at 'em: "You brood of vipers! Who warned you to flee from the wrath to come? Bear fruit that befits repentance, and do not presume to say to yourselves, 'We have Abraham as our father'; for I tell you, God is able from these stones to raise up children to Abraham. Even now the axe is laid to the root of the trees; every tree therefore that does not bear good fruit is cut down and thrown into the fire." (Matthew 3:7–10) John the Baptist had a fine theology of grace. For him we can change, if we want to— if we see the direness of not changing. The same holds true today. Only the lazy and faithless need throw in the towel. The rest know people do not live by deformation alone.

Witness

Political theology, shaking its fist under my nose, insists that our theological virtues issue in practice.[6] The issue of hope is witness. If we accept the proposition that things can go better, that there are rational warrants for leaning into the future expectantly, it is incumbent on us to put this proposition on the line, to display, enact, embody it. In terms of an existential stance, I see this making a Christian spirituality that witnesses to the ecological revolution that might be. Step by step, piece by piece, it would move us ahead and assemble a new package. Interconnectedness, naturalist prayer, non-violence, reconciliation, and hope would become habitual, postures comfortable from long use. At the core would be the realization that our part may not be to convert the nations.

We plant, Dionysius waters, and God gives the increase. I suspect that this realization, allied with a witnessing stance, can make a powerful eco-spirituality.

When we can maintain ourselves in the witnessing mode, we stand outside the usual politics of action and reaction. We may, indeed should, take such politics into pragmatic account, but our courses of action, where we put our time, energy, and money, stand free of the hurly-burly of normal politics. In terms of a biblical social ethics, we do not love other people because they have treated us well. We love other people because God has first loved us. The key to our situation is nothing so fragile, undependable, or complicated as human benevolence. The key to our situation is the good God shining forth from the face of Jesus, the creative God manifest throughout all nature. To be true to our own best perceptions of how this God has treated us and configured our world, we have to try to stride forth in faith, hope, and love.

As a consequence, we can deal with nature and ecological issues peacefully, consistently, as matters almost taken for granted. Like Daniel Berrigan speaking of the long-haul on which the peace movement has embarked, the environmentalist of Christian persuasion sets her face for a lifetime. What most matter are our stable dispositions. It is steady education, advertising, political pressuring, and ecological demonstration that wears away the rocks. Those who flare up today and are burned out tomorrow cost a movement almost as much as they gain for it. The legions that do the wholesale transforming are those whose convictions burn steadily, enlightening their lives almost without their realizing it. When we have raised a generation with a significant number of citizens whose basic passions are ecologically sound, we can expect to see significant environmental reforms. Prior to that time the crucial job is to keep the light shining, keep showing that grace still abounds. This does not make ecology less urgent, especially its nuclear dimensions. It simply sets ecology in the only foundation deep and wide enough to secure it, the overall plan of God.

As I see it, anyone persuaded by the foregoing theology of nature should emerge a committed witness to ecological or environmentalist values. Individuals may want to pursue further goals, feel called to specific causes. Well and good. One would expect this to happen, if God is at all fanning the ecological flame. But the foundation that ecology most needs goes below alternations in mood and specific projects. It is when a person finds things changed deep within that thenceforth he sees nature as a rich part of his Christian heritage—a part too precious not to guard and help prosper. Thenceforth he must oppose the legions who want to continue to exploit nature for their financial gain, firing salvo after salvo of no! The ecological ruin of nature having become one of his prime species of sin, he will brook no proposals careless of nature's rights. For, as he now sees things, nature's rights are grounded in the deepest blueprint of the divine creator. Any anthropocentrism that ignores these rights he therefore calls heretical—deeply injurious to the orthodox body.

I hope that convictions such as these, a witness such as this, will come to have great influence in our churches, legislatures, and corporate boardrooms, but that is not why I espouse it. I espouse it, I hope, because I have become convinced it is right. It makes sense in terms of what I see of the negative data, dropping down like acid rain. It makes sense in terms of what I see of the positive data, the sensible homes and sensible recyclings. So though you may outshout me at City Hall, or outclout me in Congress, you will not silence my witness. Having become convinced that environmentalism is right, I'm in for the whole journey.

Consequently, I will continue to set my facts alongside yours, set my house alongside yours, set my energy ideas alongside yours, read you my anti-nuclear manifesto. Ultimately, though, it is our selves we set alongside one another. Inevitably, the final comparison is between what the ecological and unecological lifestyles make of us who espouse them. God knows ecologists are tempted to hubris on the left and aestheticism on the right. God knows we are very imperfect. Nonetheless, few of us have a knife in the bosom of our mother or persist in ripping off the future of our children. So we do not fear fair comparisons. In fact, we welcome them. But beyond fair comparisons we will not go, for we know that violence, lying, and manipulation are the mark of our worst enemies. No, here is our little witness: earth might be fair. This is our Christian naturalism: God comes like a fresh spring breeze. Those who scarify the earth witness to darker chances. Those who love neither God nor spring breezes greatly deserve our pity.

SUMMARY AND CONCLUSION

Summary
We have been engaged in a sort of scouting-operation, trying to preview the new Christian theology of nature that today's ecological crises say we desperately need. After presenting a dramatic scenario—the advanced pollution of Cubatao, Brazil—we introduced the substance of our study by reflecting on the part that theology might play in ecological reforms. Insofar as many ecological problems boil down to deep attitudes or overall points of view that depend on religious convictions, theology (which reflects on the place of a religion in a culture) can play a significant part in the ecological controversies likely to preoccupy us in the future. If Cubatao shows us the lethal future we must labor mightily to avoid, theology can show us many of the root attitudes we must labor mightily to implant.

Part One dealt with the recent dialogue between ecology and religion. All four chapters fell into Lonergan's category of a "listening" theology, dealing mainly with reports from different camps within the ecological war zone. Overall, the effort was to gain an amateur understanding of the data and views that constitute the environmentalists' case. So, for example, Chapter One dealt with some basic issues from natural science, showing, for instance, that the laws of thermodynamics, including prominently the law of entropy, constrain any economic or cultural system to deal with nature sparingly, in recognition of the fact that nature has only a limited fund of resources. Studying "ecology" itself underscored the interconnectedness of nature's resources, while studying the current state of our waters, air, land, and animals strongly suggested that we Northern nations are living unrealistically, in patterns sure to run afoul of nature's constraints.

In Chapter Two we turned to technological and economic issues, focusing on such knotted topics as nuclear power, developing an "intermediate" or appropriate technology, non-renewable resources, renewable resources, and the debates between advocates of a steady-state economic model and their opponents who push for constant economic growth. These topics reveal the interlocking character of the various problems that "environmentalism" must target. For example, the state of the waters is inseparable from the commerce that plies the waters. The state of the air and the shape of the federal budget both show the imprints of the nuclear power industry and the defense establishment. Very quickly, therefore, one realizes that trying to develop an adequate "worldview" is not an ecological luxury. Until one gains a vantage point that places the great number of ecological factors in perspective, neither adequate understanding nor therapeutic policy is at more than the stage of gestation.

Chapter Three took us to the level of political and ethical issues. This level emphasizes the impact of society's power struggles, which often revolve around financial profit, and the role of basic views of what is right and wrong (in the best interests of the common good or likely injurious to a society's overall future). Considering the current problems of world hunger, population control, gaining recognition of nature's rights, protecting the interests of future generations, and providing for aesthetic factors exposed us to representative issues that lodge on the politico-ethical level.

Through the first three chapters, the general intent was to develop a sense of the dialectics at work in the current ecological controversies—of the implicit debates about ultimate horizons or attitudes. Chapter Four brought this dialectics closer to theology, by dealing with religious issues such as simplicity, the goddess, the impact of the ecological outlook on religious studies, sacramentalism, and reverence for life.

In Part Two we began to speak about the new Christian theology of nature that the current dialectics seems to demand. Following Lonergan's model, we outlined the main headings as the foundational, doctrinal, systematic, and practical or communications theologies a new Christian naturalism would require. Chapter Five, dealing with foundations, began with the conversion to Christ that must undergird any effective Christian reflection. Then, with special reference to ecology, it dealt with a sense of grace, nature's manifestations of God's bounty, a naturalist sacramentalism, sins against nature, and the way that religious authenticity might prove ecologically redemptive, offering the environmentalist movement numerous new beginnings.

Chapters Six and Seven, on doctrines, laid out some of the biblical and traditional theological teachings about nature. Thus we found that the law, the prophets, and the writings all offered good reasons for considering the land God's gift, and that the Pauline epistles, the synoptic gospels, and the Johannine writings further referred this gift to Christ. We also found that the early and later fathers, the medievals, the reformers, the moderns and our contemporaries have reworked the biblical data in light of the science and spirituality of their times. Seldom, however, have they overcome the somewhat anthropocentric cast of what seems to be the mainstream of the Christian tradition.

As a result, our systematics, ethics, and spirituality paid special attention to nature's independent rights. From the ontological core of our systematics, through our ethical commitment to nature's preservation, to the interrelatedness we made capital for spirituality, we strove to let nature's mystery, impersonal revelation of God, significance for future generations, and the like mount a case that God has given nature many titles to reverence.

Conclusion

Let this be the headline of our conclusion: God has given nature many titles to reverence. How might we love nature like a neighbor or relative? Let me not so much count the ways as compose a futuristic scenario, to balance what we saw at Cubatao.

From conception, a child of nature and grace would participate in an ecological culture. Blessed with an enlightened form of holistic medicine, parents would make gestation a natural process, cooperating through breathing exercises, nontoxic diets, and the like. At birth they would celebrate a divine fertility, fraught with a new generation's worth of hopes. Society at large would consider parenthood a high vocation, honoring it at least as much as latter-day hunting and gathering.

From the earliest stages of her education, a little child would absorb natural lore, educators making every effort to lead her both to care for nature's gifts and to consider all creation her home. Both parents and teachers would stress the connections among things, the mystery of their profusion and interdependence. So children might learn how to eat, clothe themselves, build shelters and the like frugally, emphasizing the free energies nature offers, the easy protections nature suggests.

For the years of adolescence and early adulthood, when our bodily energies are highest, a discerning theology of nature would promote physical fitness, more as a spiritual discipline than as a form of competition. Competition could draw forth special efforts, but the major accent would be the lifelong psychological benefits of maintaining the body in good shape. Indeed, by tuning the body and releasing psychic tensions, hard physical exercise would open a middle way between indulgence and punishment that could bring people to adulthood full of energy.

Natural sciences and technology would have an important place in the scholastic curricula dominating late youth, but a naturalist education would integrate them with humanistic and social scientific studies. Persuaded that ecology must become a staple cast of mind, such a naturalist education would want interdisciplinary approaches and teamwork to flourish, so that the university might throw off its present compartmentalization and begin again to merit its name. The result could be alumni able to deal with natural wholes holistically.

As people grew into their middle years and took up political and economic responsibilities, a naturalistic upbringing would help to free them from the isolationism and jingoism presently so debilitating. Because they had increasingly realized the unity of the earth's ecosystem, the unity of the world's economic and political systems would not seem occult. This would give liberation theology and distributive justice several openings, perhaps leading to a widespread insistence that the world's peoples really be equal with respect to both natural resources and the fruits of human labor. Steady-state economic models likely would seem to fit the earth's unitary ecosystem better than models of continued growth, so the ethical and religious obstacles to ecological health and social justice would grow dauntingly clear: How can we raise people to live by motives better than greed? What sense of beauty or justice might move the developed nations to sacrifice their superfluity for other peoples' necessities? What sense of beauty or justice might move the developing nations to generate effective programs of population control and ecological conservation?

These questions, and the still more basic question of how to stop the nuclear arms race, would remove any last doubts that the final problems are religious. At core the problem is our inhumanity: we do not do the good we should; the evil we should not we do. To overcome our evils toward nature, God the creator must give us a new heart of reverential flesh. To overcome our injustices toward one another, we must accept Christ's cross, which is God's way of conquering human evil. Throughout the lifecycle, from our first wonder at a buttercup to our last pleasure in a gentle rain, the mysteriousness of this Christian naturalism would keep growing.

One cannot put old heads on young bodies, so people near the end of the lifecycle likely would furnish the consummate poetries. Like Plato, they would know that all creatures are toys of the divine puppeteer, who creates the world for his love and play. Like Chuang Tzu, they would know that the Great Clod keeps turning, framing time in huge chunks of eternity.

To each and all they would proclaim: God doesn't so much come into our world as our world occurs in God. Christ doesn't so much redo the patterns of natural history as reveal the depths those patterns always have borne.

Thinking on these things through the seasons, the ecological Christian would keep turning. Conversion to Christ is ongoing. All turns bring us to different balconies and different airs, each of which murmurs, "Purify!" We never see nature so clearly, love Christ so dearly, follow the Spirit so nearly that we do not need to cleanse our minds, hearts, and lips with a burning coal.

A burning coal: a non-renewable resource; traditionally a primal element. Paul might have had such an Isaian creature in mind when he wrote: "For all things are yours, whether it be . . . the world or life or death or the present or the future: all these are yours, and you are Christ's and Christ is God's." (1 Cor 3:21–22) The final test of a Christian natural theology is whether it makes God's creation our home. We will have our ecological parousia, a Jerusalem of flowing water, when all things are ours, kith and kin, so that we would not dream of abusing any.

ANNOTATED BIBLIOGRAPHY

Albanese, Catherine L., *America: Religions and Religion* (Belmont, CA: Wadsworth, 1981). A solid single-volume introduction to the varieties of American religious experience.

Auel, Jean M., *The Clan of the Cave Bear* (New York: Bantam, 1981). A fascinating novel about the life of a paleolithic tribe, with a full display of their immersion in the flora and fauna of their imagined time.

Barbour, Ian G., ed., *Earth Might Be Fair: Reflections on Ethics, Religion, and Ecology* (Englewood Cliffs, NJ: Prentice-Hall, 1972). Papers, dedicated to Harold K. Schilling, by members of the Theology-and-Science Discussion Club that included Huston Smith, Daniel Day Williams, Barbour, and Schilling. Process convictions predominate.

Barbour, Ian G., ed., *Finite Resources and the Human Future* (Minneapolis: Augsburg, 1976). Food, population, resources, growth, and development considered panel-fashion by scientists, ethicians, demographers, and a U.S. senator.

Barnet, Richard J., *The Lean Years: Politics in the Age of Scarcity* (New York: Simon and Schuster, 1980). A good analysis of the energy, political, and international factors, perhaps somewhat vitiated by a horizon of enlightened self-interest.

Berger, Peter L. and Neuhaus, Richard John, eds., *Against the World for the World* (New York: Seabury, 1976). Papers from the conference that issued the 1975 Hartford Appeal against the inroads of secularism into Western civil and church life.

Caldicott, Helen, M.D., *Nuclear Madness* (Brookline, MA: Autumn Press, 1978). Facts and rhetoric from a passionate opponent of nuclear arms and nuclear power.

Callenbach, Ernest, *Ecotopia* (New York: Bantam, 1977). A novel of one possible future, were a group of ecologically determined Americans to secede from their polluted compatriots and make a different compact with nature.

Chadwick, Owen, *The Secularization of the European Mind in the Nineteenth Century* (New York: Cambridge University Press, 1975). Chadwick gave the substance of this book as the 1973–74 Gifford Lectures at Edinburgh, and it indicates how a learned, somewhat demanding historian approaches an assignment in intellectual history.

Christ, Carol P., *Diving Deep and Surfacing* (Boston: Beacon Press, 1980). A study of women's spiritual quest, as illustrated in recent feminist literature.

Cobb, John B., *Is It Too Late? A Theology of Ecology* (Beverly Hills, CA: Bruce, 1972). An early voice that delineated both the need for a new vision of nature and a sketch of that new vision in terms of process theology.

Cobb, John B., Jr. and Griffin, David Ray, *Process Theology: An Introductory Exposition* (Philadelphia: Westminster, 1976). A solid and clear exposition of process theology, well aware of ecological questions (and feminist questions, as well).

Coles, Robert, *Eskimos, Chicanos, Indians: Volume IV of Children of Crisis* (Boston: Little, Brown, 1977). Interviews with children shaped by the land much more than most American children recently have been. The Indians and Eskimos, especially, offer many hopes for the future reclamation of the cosmological myth.

Crowe, Frederick, *The Lonergan Enterprise* (Cambridge, MA: Cowley, 1980). A readable introduction to the work of the Roman Catholic theologian who has proposed perhaps the most far-reaching reform of Christian theology.

Dillard, Annie, *Pilgrim at Tinker Creek* (New York: Harper's Magazine Press, 1974). Poetic and religious musings about the cycles of nature at Tinker Creek in the Virginia Mountains. Engaging and dazzling.

Eiseley, Loren, *The Star Thrower* (New York: Harcourt Brace Jovanovich, 1978). A final collection of beautiful essays and poems by a long-time appreciator of nature.

Gremillion, Joseph, ed., *Food/Energy and the Major Faiths* (Maryknoll, NY: Orbis, 1978). Papers from the first Interreligious Peace Colloquium held at Bellagio, Italy, in 1975, that deal with the economic and demographic facts, the political problems, and the possible contributions of the world faiths.

Häring, Bernard, *Free & Faithful in Christ, Volume 3: Light to the World* (New York: Crossroad, 1981). A fine volume by perhaps the leading Roman Catholic moral theologian that deals with the responsibilities we have toward human life, both private and public. It has one of the fullest treatments of ecology I have seen by a Roman Catholic moralist.

Heilbroner, Robert L., *An Inquiry Into the Human Prospect* (New York: W. W. Norton, 1980). Heilbroner's revised version of his best-seller of the mid-1970s, distinguished by a cogent presentation of the grim facts and a skeptical horizon regarding human generosity.

Heilbroner, Robert L., *Marxism: For and Against* (New York: W. W. Norton, 1980). An illuminating introduction whose strongest suit is the author's economic background.

Herbert, Frank, *Dune* (New York: Berkeley, 1977). The first of the science fiction novels in this series, and probably the best, offering an amazing imaginative creation of a people very different from us because of their very different environment.

Hollenbach, David, *Claims in Conflict* (New York: Paulist, 1979). A fine survey of recent Roman Catholic social thought with thoughtful suggestions for its further development.

Jaki, Stanley L., *The Road of Science and the Ways to God* (Chicago: University of Chicago Press, 1978). The Gifford Lectures for 1974–75 and 1975–76, amounting to a heavily documented argument that the assumptions of Western science do not reject but rather assume the basic reality of God.

Janovy, John, *Keith County Journal* (New York: St. Martin's Press, 1978). A parasitologist from Nebraska tramps the land and convinces the rest of us that poetry is as close as a well-landed muse.

Katz, Michael, *et al.*, eds., *Earth's Answer* (New York: Lindisfarne/Harper & Row, 1977). "Explorations of Planetary Culture" from the Lindisfarne Conferences that display a very creative, if sometimes flaky, spirit of ecological renewal.

Leopold, Aldo, *A Sand County Almanac* (New York: Oxford University Press, 1966). An early classic that shows some of the beauty and joy of a life pivoted on environmentalist values—a life in which one does not think that food comes from a supermarket.

Lessing, Doris, *Canopus in Argos: Archives* (New York: Alfred A. Knopf, 1979ff). A profound meditation on humanity's current ills in the genre of science fiction.

Lonergan, Bernard J. F., *Method in Theology* (New York: Herder and Herder, 1972). Lonergan has studied the dynamics of human understanding and applied them to the study of theology, deriving eight "functional specialities" that could collaborate across disciplines.

Lossky, Vladimir, *The Mystical Theology of the Eastern Church*

(Crestwood, NY: St. Vladimir's Seminary Press, 1976). A solid presentation of Orthodox theology with special attention to its roots in deep religious experience.

Miller, G. Tyler, *Living in the Environment,* Third Edition (Belmont, CA: Wadsworth, 1982). A complete primer (college text) on ecological science and strategies. The one book I would recommend to readers who aren't interested in having more than one.

Miranda, José, *Marx and the Bible* (Maryknoll, NY: Orbis, 1974). A difficult but rewarding study of the affinities between Marxist humanism and Old Testament faith.

Nouwen, Henri, *The Way of the Heart* (New York: Seabury, 1981). A lyric adaptation of the spirituality of the desert fathers to the needs of contemporary Westerners, especially Christian ministers.

Rifkin, Jeremy, *Entropy* (New York: Bantam, 1981). Theory and analysis that place the environmental crisis in its historical setting and show the need for a new, more radically scientific world view.

Sale, Kirkpatrick, *Human Scale* (New York: Coward, McCann & Geoghegan, 1980). A full delineation of the economic, social, ecological, and political implications of "small is beautiful."

Schilling, Harold K., *The New Consciousness in Science and Religion* (Philadelphia: United Church Press, 1973). Learned, encouraging analyses by a physicist-theologian deeply sensitive to the mysteries of both science and religion.

Schumacher, E. F., *A Guide for the Perplexed* (New York: Harper & Row, 1977). The philosophy behind Schumacher's economics and ecology, which turns out to be rather traditional and religious.

Schumacher, E. F., *Good Work* (New York: Harper & Row, 1979). The last, posthumous collection of essays by the sanest, deepest spokesman for ecological and economic sanity.

Schumacher, E. F., *Small Is Beautiful: Economics As If People Mattered* (New York: Harper & Row, 1973). The seminal book by the British economist who put many of the environmentalist issues into humane perspective for the first time.

Shinn, Roger L. and Abrecht, Paul, eds., *Faith and Science in an Unjust World,* 2 Vols. (Philadelphia: Fortress, 1981). Plenary Presentations, Reports, and Recommendations from the 1979 World Council of Churches' Conference on Faith, Science, and the future held at M.I.T. An excellent set of resources.

Smith, Huston, *Forgotten Truth: The Primordial Tradition* (New York: Harper & Row, 1976). Analyses of consciousness by a leading text-writer in world religions that show the much more than technological capacities of the human brain and psyche.

Thomas, Lewis, *The Medusa and the Snail* (New York: Viking, 1979). More notes (many of them originally columns in *The New England Journal of Medicine*) of a "biology watcher" distinguished for his limpid style and eye for the interconnectedness of humans and the rest of creation. Much the same themes and high quality as in his earlier *The Lives of a Cell.*

Ward, Barbara, *Progress for a Small Planet* (New York: W. W. Norton, 1979). Solid economics, and many hopeful episodes, from a committed internationalist and defender of the futures of the poor nations.

NOTES

Introduction
   1. Warren Hoge, "Valley of Death," *The Wichita Eagle,* September 24, 1980, p. 13a (New York Times News Service).
   2. See Joseph Gremillion, *The Gospel of Peace and Justice: Catholic Social Teaching Since Pope John* (Maryknoll, NY: Orbis, 1976).
   3. See John Eagleson and Philip Scharper, eds., *Puebla and Beyond* (Maryknoll, NY: Orbis, 1979).
   4. See, for example, Timothy Ware, *The Orthodox Church* (Baltimore: Penguin, 1969), and John Meyendorff, *The Orthodox Church,* A Third Revised Edition (Crestwood, N.Y.: SVS Press, 1981).
   5. See Joseph Sittler, *Essays on Nature and Grace* (Philadelphia: Fortress, 1972); John B. Cobb, Jr., *Is It Too Late? A Theology of Ecology* (Beverly Hills, CA: Bruce, 1972).
   6. See Jerry Falwell, *Listen, America!* (Garden City, NY: Doubleday, 1980); Elizabeth Drew, "A Reporter at Large: The Interior Department," *The New Yorker,* May 4, 1981, pp. 104–138.
   7. See David Spring and Eileen Spring, eds., *Ecology and Religion in History* (New York: Harper & Row, 1974).
   8. Doris Lessing, *Canopus in Argos, Chronicles: I, Shikasta* (New York: Knopf, 1979), p. 199.

Chapter One: Issues from Natural Science
   1. G. Tyler Miller, Jr., *Living in the Environment,* Third Edition (Belmont, CA: Wadsworth, 1982). This section draws especially from pp. 3–82.
   2. Jeremy Rifkin has placed the cluster of our current global problems in this context. See his *Entropy* (New York: Bantam, 1981).
   3. Nicholas Georgescu-Roegen, "The Entropy Law and the Eco-

nomic Problem," in *Toward a Steady-State Economy,* ed. Herman E. Daly (San Francisco: W. H. Freeman, 1973), p. 46.

4. Miller, *op. cit.,* p. 44.

5. See *ibid.,* chapters 15 and 16.

6. See *ibid.,* chapter 17.

7. See *ibid.,* Enrichment Study 15.

8. See Emily Hahn, "A Reporter at Large (Endangered Species)," *The New Yorker,* September 1, 1980, p. 43, drawing on remarks of Robert Wagner, executive director of the American Association of Zoological Parks and Aquariums.

9. Miller, *op. cit.,* p. 201.

10. Hahn, *art. cit.,* p. 67, quoting William Conway, Director of the Bronx Zoo.

Chapter Two: Technological and Economic Issues

1. See Jacques Ellul, *The Technological System* (New York: Seabury, 1980), and *Perspectives on Our Age* (New York: Seabury, 1981).

2. Ellul, *Perspectives on Our Age,* pp. 83–84.

3. See Amory B. Lovins, "Guest Editorial: Technology Is the Answer (But What Was the Question?)," in Miller, *op. cit.,* pp. 290–292.

4. Hannes Alfven, "Guest Editorial: War: The Worst Environmental Threat," *ibid.,* p. 17.

5. Helen Caldicott, *Nuclear Madness* (Brookline, MA: Autumn Press, 1978), p. 65.

6. Data in this paragraph are from Caldicott, *ibid.,* pp. 70–71. See also Fred C. Shapiro, "A Reporter at Large (Radioactive Waste)," *The New Yorker,* October 19, 1981, pp. 53–139.

7. See E. F. Schumacher, *Good Work* (New York: Harper & Row, 1979), pp. 5–61. By comparison with most essays on technology (e.g., those of the *Daedalus* issue [109/1: Winter, 1980] entitled *Modern Technology: Problem or Opportunity*), Schumacher's are outstanding for their clarity, depth, humaneness, and comprehensiveness. In my opinion, he well deserves his prophet's mantle. See also his *Small Is Beautiful* (New York: Harper & Row, 1973) and *A Guide for the Perplexed* (New York: Harper & Row, 1977).

8. E. F. Schumacher, *Good Work,* pp. 60–61.

9. For more on this, see Kirkpatrick Sale, *Human Scale* (New York: Coward, McCann, & Geoghegan, 1980).

10. Richard Barnet, "A Reporter at Large (The World's Resources—Part I)," *The New Yorker,* March 17, 1980, p. 47.

11. Richard Barnet, "A Reporter at Large (The World's Resources—Part II)," *The New Yorker,* March 31, 1980, p. 41.

12. *Ibid.*

13. See Miller, *op. cit.,* p. 245.

14. See Robert L. Heilbroner, *An Inquiry into the Human Prospect* (New York: W. W. Norton, 1980).

15. See Miller, *op. cit.,* pp. 307, 311. I have corrected Miller's upper limit figure for 80% U.S. oil depletion, which in the text is 2105, to 2015, which better squares with his own chart.

16. For a somewhat contrary view, see John L. Simon, "The Scarcity of Raw Materials: A Challenge to the Conventional Wisdom," *The Atlantic,* 247/6 (June 1981), pp. 33–41.

17. See Miller, *op. cit.,* pp. 271–273.

18. *Ibid.,* p. 271.

19. See Tracy Kidder, "The Future of the Photovoltaic Cell," *The Atlantic,* 245/6 (June 1980), pp. 68–76.

20. See Miller, *op. cit.,* 258–260.

21. Herman E. Daly, "The Ecological and Moral Necessity for Limiting Economic Growth," in *Faith and Science in an Unjust World,* Vol. 1, ed. Roger L. Shinn (Philadelphia: Fortress, 1980), pp. 212–220.

22. *Ibid.,* p. 212.

23. Jorgen Randers and Donella Meadows, "The Carrying Capacity of Our Global Environment," in *Toward a Steady-State Economy,* p. 283.

24. See Daly, "The Ecological and Moral Necessity for Limiting Economic Growth," p. 213.

Chapter Three: Political and Ethical Issues

1. Diogo de Gaspar, "Economics and World Hunger," in *Faith and Science in an Unjust World,* Vol. 1, p. 225.

2. See Sudhir Sen, "How to Combat World Famine," *Commonweal,* CVIII/16 (September 11, 1981), pp. 489–496.

3. *Ibid.,* p. 490.

4. *Ibid.*

5. For further background on the Green Revolution, see Norman Borlaug, "The Fight Against Hunger," in *Finite Resources and the Human Future,* ed. Ian G. Barbour (Minneapolis: Augsburg, 1976), pp. 63–91.

6. See Geoffrey Barraclough, ed., *The Times Atlas of World History* (Maplewood, N.J.: Hammond, 1979), pp. 208–209.

7. Teresa A. Sullivan, "Numbering Our Days Aright: Human Longevity and the Problem of Intimacy," in *Toward Vatican III,* ed. D. Tracy, H. Küng, and J. Metz (New York: Seabury, 1978), p. 284.

8. *Ibid.,* pp. 284–285.

9. De Gaspar, *art. cit.,* p. 225.

10. *Ibid.,* p. 226.

11. Barbara Ward, *Progress for a Small Planet* (New York: W. W. Norton, 1979), p. 181.

12. Bernard Häring, *Free & Faithful in Christ,* Vol. 3 (New York: Crossroad, 1981), pp. 15–16. Häring refers to P. Ehrlich and A. Ehrlich, *Population and Environment: Issues in Human Ecology* (San Francisco: W. H. Freeman, 1970), as an example of "enormous exaggerations and unproven presuppositions," but he cites no particulars, offers no counter figures, to back up this near character assassination. In this the sort of ethical example our leading moral theologians should be giving?

13. *Ibid.,* p. 181.

14. Paul W. Taylor, "The Ethics of Respect for Nature," *Environmental Ethics,* 3/3 (Fall 1981), p. 211. See also R. and V. Routley, "Against the Inevitability of Human Chauvinism," *Ethics and Problems of the 21st Century,* ed. K. E. Goodpaster and K. M. Sayre (Notre Dame, IN: University of Notre Dame Press, 1979), pp. 36–59.

15. *Ibid.,* p. 216.

16. Anthony J. Povilis, "On Assigning Rights to Animals and Nature," *Environmental Ethics,* 2/1 (Spring 1980), pp. 67–71.

17. See the publication of the American Academy of Arts and Sciences, *When Values Conflict* (Boston: Ballinger, 1976).

18. See Julian Huxley, *The Human Crisis* (Seattle: University of Washington Press, 1963), p. 24.

19. Robert L. Heilbroner, *An Inquiry into the Human Prospect,* p. 179.

20. *Ibid.,* pp. 181–182.

21. Gabriel Nahas, "Genetic Meddling," in *Faith and Science in an Unjust World,* Vol. 1, p. 281.

22. *Ibid.,* p. 282.

23. See Michael Polanyi, *Personal Knowledge* (New York: Harper & Row, 1964), especially pp. 69–245.

24. Ian G. Barbour, ed., *Earth Might Be Fair* (Englewood Cliffs, NJ: Prentice-Hall, 1972).

25. See Paolo Soleri, "The City of the Future," in *Earth's Answer,* ed. M. Katz, W. Marsh, and G. Gordon Thompson (New York:

NOTES

Lindisfarne/Harper & Row, 1977), pp. 72–77, and Sean Wellesley-Miller, "Towards a Symbiotic Architecture," *ibid.*, pp. 78–94.

26. See E. F. Schumacher, *Small Is Beautiful,* pp. 50–58.

27. Lewis Thomas, *The Medusa and the Snail* (New York: Viking, 1979), pp. 7–11.

28. Robert C. North, *The World That Could Be* (Stanford, CA: The Portable Stanford, 1976).

29. See Lewis S. Ford, *The Lure of God* (Philadelphia: Fortress, 1978).

30. See Chang Chung-yuan, *Creativity and Taoism* (New York: Harper & Row, 1963).

31. See William LaFleur, "Saigyo and the Buddhist Value of Nature," *History of Religions,* 13 (1973–1974), pp. 93–128, 227–248.

32. Pictures of these shrines, and commentaries, are available in Denise Lardner Carmody and John Tully Carmody, *Ways to the Center: An Introduction to World Religions* (Belmont, CA: Wadsworth, 1981), as are discussions of how "nature" functions in each world religion's general outlook.

33. See for example Yasunari Kawabata, *The Sound of the Mountain* (Rutland, VT: Tuttle, 1971).

34. Huston Smith, "Tao Now: An Ecological Testament," in *Earth Might Be Fair,* pp. 62–81.

Chapter Four: Religious Issues

1. See Robert McAfee Brown, *Gustavo Gutierrez* (Atlanta: John Knox, 1980).

2. Bernard Häring, *op. cit.,* p. 183.

3. See Paul Santmire, "Ecology, Justice, and Theology," *The Christian Century,* 92/17 (May 12, 1976), pp. 46–464.

4. Marie Augusta Neal, *A Socio-Theology of Letting Go* (New York: Paulist, 1977).

5. C. T. Kurien, "A Third World Perspective," in *Faith and Science in an Unjust World,* Vol. 1, p. 221.

6. John A. Ryan, *Distributive Justice* (New York: Macmillan, 1927), p. 397.

7. See, for example, Helen and Scott Nearing, *Living the Good Life* (New York: Schocken, 1970).

8. See Ernest Callenbach, *Ecotopia* (New York: Bantam, 1977).

9. See Annie Dillard, *Pilgrim at Tinker Creek* (New York: Harper's Magazine Press, 1974).

10. Thomas Merton, *The Way of Chuang Tzu* (New York: New

ECOLOGY AND RELIGION

Directions, 1965), pp. 60–61.

11. See Rita M. Gross, ed., *Beyond Androcentrism* (Missoula, MT: Scholars Press, 1977).

12. Carol P. Christ, *Diving Deep and Surfacing* (Boston: Beacon Press, 1980), p. 22. The quotation from de Beauvoir is from *The Second Sex* (New York: Bantam, 1970), p. 341.

13. See Sherry B. Ortner, "Is Female to Male as Nature Is to Culture?" in *Woman, Culture and Society,* ed. M. Z. Rosaldo and L. Lamphere (Stanford, CA: Stanford University Press, 1974), pp. 67–87, and Carol MacCormack and Marilyn Strathern, eds., *Nature, Culture and Gender* (New York: Cambridge University Press, 1980).

14. See Naomi R. Goldenberg, *Changing of the Gods* (Boston: Beacon, 1979), especially pp. 96–99.

15. See, for example, Stella Kramrisch, "The Indian Great Goddess," *History of Religions,* 14/4 (May 1975), pp. 235–265. For an overview of all the religions, see Denise Lardner Carmody, *Women and World Religions* (Nashville, TN: Abingdon, 1979).

16. Starhawk (Miriam Simos), *The Spiral Dance: A Rebirth of the Ancient Religion of the Great Goddess* (San Francisco: Harper & Row, 1979), p. 78.

17. Rosemary Ruether, *New Woman, New Earth* (New York: Seabury, 1975), p. 204. For Dinnerstein's more psychoanalytically oriented views, see *The Mermaid and the Minotaur* (New York: Harper & Row, 1976), especially pp. 207–277.

18. Clifford Geertz, *Agricultural Involution: The Processes of Ecological Change in Indonesia* (Berkeley: University of California Press, 1963), pp. 7–8. His work on Islam is *Islam Observed* (Chicago: University of Chicago Press, 1968).

19. See Ake Hultkrantz, "An Ecological Approach to Religion," *Ethnos,* 31 (1966), pp. 131–150, and "Ecology of Religion: Its Scope and Methodology," *Review of Ethnology,* 4 (1974), pp. 1–12. Hultkrantz's major work, *The Religions of the American Indians* (Berkeley: University of California Press, 1979), was originally published (in Swedish) in 1967 and seems, in conception, less than a full instance of this ecological approach.

20. Bruce Lincoln, *Priests, Warriors, and Cattle: A Study in the Ecology of Religions* (Berkeley: University of California Press, 1981), p. 10. The quotation from Hultkrantz is from "An Ecological Approach to Religion," pp. 147–148.

21. See, for instance, Barre Toelken, "Seeing with a Native Eye," in *Seeing with a Native Eye,* ed. Walter Holden Capps (New York:

Harper & Row, 1976), pp. 9–24, and Robert Coles, *Eskimos, Chicanos, Indians: Volume IV of Children of Crisis* (Boston: Little, Brown and Company, 1977), pp. 395–554.

22. See Robert L. Cohn, *The Shape of Sacred Space: Four Biblical Studies* (Chico, CA: Scholars Press, 1981). See especially pp. 7–23, where the influence of cultural anthropology (Victor Turner's "liminality") is strongest.

23. Denise Lardner Carmody, *The Oldest God: Archaic Religion Yesterday and Today* (Nashville, TN: Abingdon, 1981).

24. See Häring, *op. cit.,* pp. 178–179.

25. See Mary Collins, "Critical Questions for Liturgical Theology," *Worship,* 53/4 (July 1979), especially pp. 305–306.

26. Joseph Keenan, "The Importance of the Creation Motif in a Eucharistic Prayer," *ibid.,* p. 349.

27. Raymond Vaillancourt, *Toward A Renewal of Sacramental Theology* (Collegeville, MN: Liturgical Press, 1979), p. 70.

28. Alexander Schmemman, *Introduction to Liturgical Theology,* Second Edition (Crestwood, NY: SVS Press, 1975), p. 23.

29. See M. Basil Pennington, *O Holy Mountain!* (Garden City, NY: Doubleday, 1978).

30. See Edward A. Armstrong, *Saint Francis: Nature Mystic* (Berkeley: University of California Press, 1974).

31. See Raymond Panikkar, *The Trinity and the Religious Experience of Man* (Maryknoll, NY: Orbis, 1974).

32. See Erik Erikson, *Gandhi's Truth* (New York: W. W. Norton, 1969), and "Reflections on Dr. Borg's Life Cycle," in *Adulthood,* ed. Erik Erikson (New York: W. W. Norton, 1978), pp. 1–31.

33. Garrett Hardin, "Life Boat Ethics," in *Finite Resources and the Human Future,* p. 41.

34. Roger L. Shinn, "Life Boat Ethics: A Response," *ibid.,* p. 51.

35. Garrett Hardin, "Ecology and the Death of Providence," *Zygon,* 15/1 (March 1980), p. 66. See also his *Promethean Ethics: Living with Death, Competition, and Triage* (Seattle: University of Washington Press, 1980).

Chapter Five: Foundational Reflections

1. See Walter E. Conn, ed., *Conversion* (New York: Alba House, 1978). Emilie Griffin's *Turning* (Garden City, N.Y.: Doubleday, 1980) is an enlightening personal account.

2. See Lawrence Cunningham, *The Meaning of Saints* (San Francisco: Harper & Row, 1980).

3. Karl Rahner, *Foundations of Christian Faith* (New York: Seabury, 1978); Edward Schillebeeckx, *Christ* (New York: Seabury, 1980). See also Leo O'Donovan, ed., *A World of Grace* (New York: Seabury, 1980).

4. Lucas Grollenberg, *Jesus* (Philadelphia: Westminster, 1978).

5. Karl Barth, *Church Dogmatics,* III/4 (Edinburgh: T. & T. Clark, 1961), p. 336.

6. Paul Tillich, *Systematic Theology,* I (Chicago: University of Chicago Press, 1967), p. 262.

7. See Ruth M. Underhill, *Red Man's Religion* (Chicago: University of Chicago Press, 1965).

8. David Tracy, *The Analogical Imagination* (New York: Crossroad, 1981), pp. 202–18.

9. See Timothy Ware, *The Orthodox Church* (Baltimore: Penguin, 1969), pp. 281–303.

Chapter Six: Biblical Doctrines

1. Herbert May, "Fertile Crescent and Its Environment," *The Interpreter's One-Volume Commentary on the Bible,* ed. Charles M. Laymon (Nashville: Abingdon, 1971), p. 1003.

2. Brevard S. Childs, *Introduction to the Old Testament as Scripture* (Philadelphia: Fortress, 1979), p. 155.

3. Samuel Terrien, *The Elusive Presence* (New York: Harper & Row, 1978), p. 392.

4. Walter Brueggemann, *The Land* (Philadelphia: Fortress, 1977), p. 185.

5. *Ibid.,* p. 12.

6. *Ibid.,* p. 104.

7. Eric Voegelin, *Order and History, I* (Baton Rouge: Louisiana State University Press, 1956), p. 504.

8. Claus Westermann, *The Psalms* (Minneapolis: Augsburg, 1980), p. 97.

9. *Ibid.,* pp. 98–99.

10. Marvin H. Pope, *The Anchor Bible Job* (Garden City, N.Y.: Doubleday, 1965), p. lxxvii.

11. W. D. Davies, *The Gospel and the Land* (Berkeley: University of California Press, 1974), p. 166.

12. *Ibid.,* p. 179.

13. Joseph Fitzmyer, "The Letter to the Romans," *The Jerome Biblical Commentary,* II, ed. R. Brown, J. Fitzmyer, and R. Murphy (Englewood Cliffs, N.J.: Prentice-Hall, 1968), p. 296.

14. Edwin Cyril Blackman, "The Letter of Paul to the Romans," *The Interpreter's One-Volume Commentary on the Bible,* p. 770.

15. William Barclay, *The Letters to the Philippians, Colossians, and Thessalonians,* Rev. Ed. (Philadelphia: Westminister, 1975), p. 120.

16. *Ibid.,* p. 123.

17. See W. D. Davies, *The Gospel and the Land,* pp. 255–56.

18. Pheme Perkins, *Hearing the Parables of Jesus* (Ramsey, N.J.: Paulist, 1981), pp. 76–89.

19. *Ibid.,* p. 89.

20. W. D. Davies, *The Gospel and the Land,* p. 333.

21. See J. L. Houlden, *Ethics and the New Testament* (New York: Oxford University Press, 1977).

22. See Leander E. Keck, *The New Testament Experience of Faith* (St. Louis: Bethany, 1976).

23. James Barr, "Man and Nature: The Ecological Controversy and the Old Testament," in *Ecology and Religion in History,* ed. D. Spring and E. Spring (New York: Harper & Row, 1974), pp. 48–75.

Chapter Seven: Traditional Theological Doctrines

1. See Jaroslav Pelikan, *The Christian Tradition, I* (Chicago: University of Chicago Press, 1971), pp. 37–38.

2. Ernst Troeltsch, *The Social Teaching of the Christian Churches, I* (Chicago: University of Chicago Press, 1981), p. 150.

3. Pelikan, *op. cit.,* pp. 294–95.

4. See G. W. H. Lampe, "Christian Theology in the Patristic Age," in *A History of Christian Doctrine,* ed. H. Cunliffe-Jones & B. Drewery (Philadelphia: Fortress, 1980), pp. 170–180.

5. *Ibid.,* p. 94.

6. Etienne Gilson, *A Gilson Reader* (Garden City, N.Y.: Doubleday, 1957), p. 265.

7. Jaroslav Pelikan, *The Christian Tradition, II* (Chicago: University of Chicago Press, 1974), p. 248.

8. See Vladimir Lossky, *The Mystical Theology of the Eastern Church* (Crestwood, NY: St. Vladimir's Seminary Press, 1976).

9. Benjamin Drewery, "Martin Luther," in *A History of Christian Doctrine,* p. 332.

10. John T. McNeil, *The History and Character of Calvinism* (New York: Oxford University Press, 1979), p. 209.

11. Jaroslav Pelikan, *The Christian Tradition, II,* pp. 291–292.

12. See Ronald W. Hepburn, "Nature, Philosophical Ideas of," in

The Encyclopedia of Philosophy, ed. Paul Edwards, V (New York: Macmillan, 1967), pp. 454–458.

13. Stanley Jaki, *The Road of Science and the Ways to God* (Chicago: University of Chicago Press, 1978).

14. William A. Clebsch, *American Religious Thought* (Chicago: University of Chicago Press, 1973), pp. 52–53.

15. *Ibid.,* p. 161.

16. Charles Birch, "Nature, Humanity and God in Ecological Perspective," in *Faith and Science in an Unjust World,* I. ed. Roger Shinn (Philadelphia: Fortress, 1980), p. 62.

17. J. Deretz and A. Nocent, eds., *Dictionary of the Council* (Washington: Corpus Books, 1968).

18. John Paul II, *Sources of Renewal* (San Francisco: Harper & Row, 1980), pp. 46–47. DV refers to *Dei Verbum,* the Vatican II decree on revelation.

Chapter Eight: A Systematic Approach

1. See Loren Eiseley, "The Lethal Factor," in his *The Star Thrower* (New York: Harcourt Brace Jovanovich, 1978), pp. 251–66.

2. See Bernard Lonergan, *Insight: A Study of Human Understanding* (New York: Philosophical Library, 1957).

3. See Eric Voegelin, *Order and History, IV* (Baton Rouge: Louisiana State University Press, 1974); John Carmody, "Voegelin's Noetic Differentiation: Religious Implications," *Horizons,* 8/2 (Fall 1981), 223–246.

4. Eric Voegelin, *Order and History, IV,* pp. 333–334.

5. See Lewis S. Ford, *The Lure of God* (Philadelphia: Fortress, 1978); Langdon Gilkey, *Reaping the Whirlwind* (New York: Seabury, 1976); John B. Cobb, Jr. and David Ray Griffin, *Process Theology: An Introductory Exposition* (Philadelphia: Westminster, 1976).

6. Wilfred Cantwell Smith, *Towards a World Theology* (Philadelphia: Westminster, 1981).

7. Karl Rahner, *Foundations of Christian Faith* (New York: Seabury, 1978), pp. 153–161.

8. See Frederick Buechner's wonderful novel, *Godric* (New York: Atheneum, 1981).

9. See Eric Voegelin, *Order and History, I* (Baton Rouge: Louisiana State University Press, 1956), pp. 1–110.

10. As beginning ventures, see Doris Lessing, *Canopus in Argos* (New York: Alfred A. Knopf, 1977ff) and Ernest Callenbach, *Ecotopia*

(New York: Bantam, 1977). See also John Shea, *Stories of God* (Chicago: Thomas More, 1978).

Chapter Nine: Ethical Implications
    1. For a good feminist complement to these reflections, see Elizabeth Dodson Gray, *Green Paradise Lost* (Wellesley, MA: Roundtable Press, 1981).
    2. See Erik H. Erikson, ed., *Adulthood* (New York: W. W. Norton, 1978).
    3. See Robert L. Heilbroner, *An Inquiry into the Human Prospect* (New York: W. W. Norton, 1980), pp. 179–186.
    4. See Karl Rahner, *Foundations of Christian Faith* (New York: Seabury, 1978), pp. 457–459.
    5. G. Tyler Miller, Jr., *Living in the Environment,* Third Edition (Belmont, CA: Wadsworth, 1982), pp. 136–137.
    6. Carl Djerassi, *The Politics of Contraception,* II (Stanford, CA: Stanford Alumni Association, 1979), p. 225.
    7. G. Tyler Miller, Jr., *op. cit.,* p. 211.
    8. See Marie Augusta Neal, *A Socio-Theology of Letting Go* (New York: Paulist, 1977); Bernard Häring, *Free and Faithful in Christ, III* (New York: Crossroad, 1981), pp. 169–208.
    9. See Jacques Ellul, *The Technological System* (New York: Continuum, 1980).

Chapter Ten: Implications for Spirituality
    1. Colin M. Turnbull, *The Mountain People* (New York: Simon & Schuster, 1972).
    2. Colin M. Turnbull, *The Forest People* (New York: Simon & Schuster, 1962).
    3. See Elise Boulding, *Women in the Twentieth Century World* (New York: Sage Publications, 1977).
    4. Barbara Ward, *Progress for a Small Planet* (New York: W. W. Norton, 1979), p. 64.
    5. *Ibid.*
    6. See Rosemary Radford Ruether, *To Change the World* (New York: Crossroad, 1981), and Tom F. Driver, *Christ in a Changing World* (New York: Crossroad, 1981).